William Tyndale

The Smuggler's Flame

William Tyndale

The Smuggler's Flame

Lori Rich

CF4·K

Copyright © 2004 Lori Rich
This edition printed in 2018
Paperback ISBN: 978-1-5271-0174-6
ebook ISBN: 978-1-5271-0226-2
mobi ISBN: 978-1-5271-0227-9

First printed in 2004 and reprinted in 2009
ISBN 978-1-85792-972-0

Published by Christian Focus Publications,
Geanies House, Fearn, Tain, Ross-shire, IV20 1TW, Scotland,
United Kingdom.
www.christianfocus.com
email: info@christianfocus.com

Bible Studies; Discussion topics; Timeline and Life Summary
Copyright ©2004 Christian Focus Publications
Cover design by Daniel van Straaten
Cover illustration by Fred Apps
Printed and bound by Nørhaven, Denmark

Scripture quotes are based on the King James and Tyndale Bible.
Bible Studies refer to the New International Version copyright
© 1973, 1978, 1984 International Bible Society.

Quotes from common domain have been used throughout this
book but some have been modernised for ease of understanding.

Contents

To my husband Jim, for whom the Reformers are
more than a dusty old time period,
but a way of life today.

To Tammy, without whose help the book would not
have been possible.

And to my mom, who, like Tyndale, has had
every reason in a sometimes hard life
to doubt God, and has never once considered
that an option.

Against the Tide

It was a dark, murky night in London. Fog wrapped around the city walls. It lay over rooftops and wound along dark alleyways, snaking through the city streets. Misting up along the River Thames like a long woollen blanket, it turned seeing men into blind ones beneath its thick cover. It was hard to see your hand in front of your face.

In one corner of the city, in a small, modest, white wooden house, a night watchman looked at himself in the mirror, adjusted his black worker's cap, and brushed the specks of dirt from his dark blue shirt. Just preparing for an evening of night watch, he gave a proud, contemptuous sniff at the mirror.

'Lawbreakers,' he scoffed peevishly at it, a ratty, malevolent gleam in his eye. 'If I catch you,' he said angrily, shaking a long, gaunt finger for emphasis, 'you'll be sorry you were ever born. King Henry's orders,' he added importantly.

Meanwhile, as he spoke, five miles away a boat with books came sliding smoothly up the river. Packed just that morning at the back of the print shop, stuffed in unmarked packing crates, the books now sat on the boat, jammed underneath and in between wooden boxes, cider barrels and an old, crusty, weatherbeaten wheel.

'Thought we were going to get caught last night,' one burly man with scraggly, unkempt red hair said nervously to the man next to him.

'I feel like that every night,' the second man's thick, husky voice replied, as he eyed the banks of the river uneasily.

'Gotta feed the wife and kids,' the first said. 'Otherwise I wouldn't be here.'

'Me neither,' the second man agreed, nodding vigorously. 'You can bet the king's gold on that.'

The boat continued to creep stealthily along, slinking quietly past the dark alleyways and buildings that stacked up against the London banks of the River Thames.

In a short time, it glided through the darkness and slid smoothly by entrances to tunnels that ran underneath London Bridge. Things in the boat were very quiet now. This was dangerous country.

The night had a gloomy half-light, with very little moon. Clouds masked the sky. The city, too, seemed eerily quiet. A lone dog howled in the distance and what little moon there was now whisked behind the cloak of dark clouds.

Slap, slap. Tonight's only sound was the thin ripple of water made by the boat's smooth bow, and the clap of the River Thames beating back against its side.

'Quiet night tonight, eh?' the burly man whispered low to his friend.

'Too quiet,' the other whispered back. 'I don't like it.'

'Shhhh,' said a third, very nasty voice. 'You'll get us all killed.'

They saw the shoreline near. As the boat drew closer, all eyes on the boat now peered intently towards it. Hawk-like, they scanned up and down the long line of misty bank – the streets, the docks, the houses – for any sign of movement, for anything unusual or odd, for anything that smelled of the royal crown. Their cargo was due at port at the scheduled time and seemed like legitimate business.

But underneath cloth and rye and cornmeal and other merchant goods the smuggled books sat. Of course, barrels two and four housed only cloth and cornmeal, if the night watchman asked.

In most of the houses the curtains were drawn, but a light was on in one. From a second storey window, a woman peered out, her glance following the boat's sly movements with interest. The crew eyed one another nervously. Still, you couldn't let your nerves jangle at everything or you would never survive.

Finally the boat pulled up to port, long tendrils of seaweed still clinging to its wooden sides. The captain stepped off and looked around while men unpacked the crates and tried hard to look and act normal, whatever that meant.

Footsteps now approached, clomping along the wooden pier. One of the men started. Rats! It was the night watchman; he was out tonight. The shiphands had been hoping it would be quiet.

'Dark night, ain't she?' he said briskly, coming alongside one of the workers, his thin, gaunt face now yellow-grey in the fog. One worker, a huge man, with arms the size of iron posts, grunted. None of the workers looked at each other.

'So, what are we unloading here this evening?' the night watchman sniffed with an angry scowl. Leaning over the nearest crate, he drummed his fingers on it impatiently and deliberately. His eyes narrowed with suspicion. He had only one thing on his mind, and it wasn't chit-chat.

'Oh, you know, the usual,' the huge man now replied, trying to sound very, very casual. 'Just cloth and cornmeal. Would you like to take a look?' He was calling the night watchman's bluff, hoping it would set him off course. He tried not to blink too much. Blinking was a dead giveaway.

'No, that's all right,' the night watchman retorted curtly, toying with his victim. 'I'm tired tonight …' Still, one could see, even by the moon's stingy light, his purpled face contorted, bulging. He stepped forward menacingly.

'You know,' he said gleefully, 'on second thought, I really should take a look. After all, the King has not been happy about books that have been coming into our country.' He pronounced the word 'happy' as if it were a disease. He had a cold, cruel voice. 'And when the King's not happy …, ' He paused then pronounced testily, 'nobody's happy. Open her up,' he ordered, pointing a lean, bony finger at the barrels.

'Sir?'

'Open her up, I said.'

The shiphand's stomach lurched but his eyes remained calm. He felt around for the barrel with the wooden edge – barrel two – and prayed he had the right one.

Not a praying man by nature, the shiphand now crammed a hundred thousand prayers into those few long seconds. All eyes were riveted on him, frozen.

Gingerly and slowly, he prised open the crate's lid, using a long, thick iron bar. When he did so, cloth – cloth of every colour and kind – rich, ruby-coloured damasks, smooth deep plum velvets, and more ordinary white everyday woollens – began to flutter loosely in the night air. The shiphand breathed a sigh of relief inside. His heart thumped back into rhythm.

Outwardly, he never let on a thing. 'You see? Just like I said,' he groused convincingly back at the watchman. 'Cloth. A late shipment. Have to keep the merchants happy, you know.' He watched the night watchman's dark narrow eyes closely and spoke with an even, calm voice. 'It's going to be all right,' he kept telling himself.

'Hmmpf,' the night watchman grunted gruffly, rubbing the back of his neck, still looking suspiciously unhappy. 'All right then, keep it moving. Bring it in,' he growled begrudgingly. He turned on his heel and stomped back down the street, the uneven slap of his footsteps receding into the darkness.

Meanwhile, underneath the cloth in other barrels the stowaway books lay undetected – safe for this evening. They had made it – this time, but the men's future and the future of the books remained uncertain. Why? Why all the fuss about a few spindly little books? Because these books weren't just any old books. They were the books of William Tyndale.

'I'm sure that they'd love to get their hands on him,' the burly shiphand said, only after the crates had been unloaded and the ship had pulled away from the shore.

'On who?' the other replied.

'William Tyndale.'

'Who's he, anyway?'

'He's the one who wrote and translated all these books. He must be pretty important if England is going to all this trouble to find him.'

'And pretty smart, if he can write this much.'

'Well, all I know is I'm just glad we kept our own skins tonight. I'm telling you, my heart can't take much more of this. I really need to quit and become a barber or something …'

'I know what you mean.'

Trouble in Gloucestershire

Five years earlier, one warm, dark night in Gloucestershire, England, William Tyndale, a man of about twenty-five, sat in his room, hunched over his desk. Stretching his legs and unfolding a piece of parchment, he thought about all the work he had to do and the correspondence he had to catch up on. On the other side of the desk sat piles of papers and parchments for tomorrow's tutoring lessons, for William Tyndale was a tutor to a wealthy landed family there, the family of Sir John Walsh.

Just then the moon shone through the clouds, casting a soft light over the acreage that was the Walshes' land, and Tyndale reflected gratefully that he had a place to live and work, and especially a place as splendid as Little Sodbury Manor. It gave him money in his pocket, a place to live and food from the family table. He was glad, after his schooling, that he had found employment here.

In the distance he thought he heard the sound of the children laughing, playing, elsewhere in the house.

Still, employment meant work and he needed to work hard this evening to catch up on some tasks. He put the letter down and picked up the notes for tomorrow. But just as his mind began to concentrate again on his notes and parchments he heard another noise, an unusual one. He stopped suddenly. Had he heard right? Were they footsteps skittering along the corridor outside his room? Yes they were. He then heard a quick, sharp rap at the door. The sound startled him into dropping an uncurled piece of parchment onto the floor. An urgent, insistent voice then called out to him from behind it. Tyndale nearly jumped out of his skin.

'William, William,' a voice whispered through the keyhole, 'can you hear me? Have you heard? You must come at once!' Tyndale knew instantly it was Lady Anne, wife of Sir John Walsh, his employer. But her voice sounded concerned, frightened even, and as he moved quickly over to the door he wondered – what could be the matter? It was not normal for the lady of the house to call upon him so urgently. As he bent towards the door handle he could hear her breath coming in gasps – she'd been running. Something was very wrong indeed.

Tyndale's heart skipped a beat and he quickly flung the door open to find himself staring into a flushed, red face, paralysed with fear. The flame from William's candle flickered with the sudden rush of air from the door. Lady Anne looked faint. 'What is it, Lady Anne? ' he gasped. The fear on the woman's face was so strong Tyndale knew that someone's life was in danger – perhaps it was his? 'Breathe,' he told himself, 'breathe.' But it was hard to breathe. Lady Anne, always polite and well-ordered, was standing before him dishevelled and obviously terrified.

'What is it?' he said. 'What is it?'

'Follow me, William, and hurry,' she gasped out. 'Someone has come to see you – he cannot stay long – and the news is not good.' Lady Anne then turned and fled down the long dark corridor. Her skirts rustled in the darkness as she disappeared into the shadows.

'My family, is it my family?' he yelled down the corridor after her as she took off.

'No,' she yelled back. 'Come with me.'

Racing along the corridor behind her, he asked anxiously, 'Is someone hurt? What is it?' But Lady Anne seemed more interested in hurrying him to the Great Hall than telling him any actual facts about what was going on. What was going on? Tyndale asked himself. They wound their way quickly down the narrow stairs, and as they ran their shadows cast large uneven shapes on the walls and woven tapestries. In seconds the pair had reached the Great Hall, and by then it wasn't just Lady Anne who was out of breath. Tyndale stood gasping by the door – struggling to get enough breath to ask his employer why he was running.

'What is it?' he finally gasped, bending over to catch his breath. 'Tell me *something,*' he pleaded.

'I'm sorry, William,' Lady Anne whispered. 'It's just that the man who has come to see you said he has only a few minutes or his life may be in danger. He seems very nervous.'

'What? What is it? Do you know?' he asked her.

'Killings, killings,' she whispered back. 'Something about killings. I'm not sure. But here,' she gestured towards the door. 'He can tell you as well as I can.'

'William,' she said, turning around as he took a step towards the room. 'Please speak quietly so the children don't hear anything. You understand, don't you?'

'Of course,' Tyndale nodded reassuringly.

Lady Anne then disappeared down the corridor, thinking only of keeping her boisterous, curious children out of earshot.

Tyndale, meanwhile, a little dazed, took another deep breath and exhaled slowly. There. That helped a little. He could almost breathe again. Breathing was good.

Taking a cautious step into the Great Hall, he found the guest already waiting for him there, sitting in a wooden armchair near the fire, which was crackling low and orange-red in the grate. The guest, a large, thick, sturdy-looking man dressed in a cloak with a dark brown hood, had deep-set eyes, eyes that looked even deeper in the shadows thrown by the flames. The man started when he heard the slap of Tyndale's feet against the hard, cold floor.

'You have come to see me?' Tyndale prompted, now stepping further into the room, just underneath the thin, spiky, wrought-iron chandelier. 'Tell me, friend, what is it? What have you come to see me about?'

The man stood up from where he was crouching by the flickering fire, while the glowing light cast eerie shadows on the portrait hanging above it. Looking angrily and helplessly towards Tyndale, he took off his hood. 'I'm afraid,' he said. 'Afraid they will kill my friends.'

For all the running and the fear Tyndale was still none the wiser. 'It's all right,' he said, slowly and patiently, 'Slow down and tell me. Who? Who are you afraid for?'

The man's hand trembled as he spoke. 'Husbands – fathers – brothers,' he said, pausing. 'My friends,' he said grimly. 'The authorities have taken them in for questioning. You know what happened a few years ago in Coventry, don't you? The authorities put people to death for teaching their children the Lord's Prayer and other parts of the Bible in English.' He paused. 'My friends have taught their children these things as well. We believe in knowing and understanding the Word of God.' He paused. 'I don't know what the authorities know, but my friends have been taken in for questioning, even as we speak. I am afraid for them …'

The man looked at the floor.

Tyndale nodded sadly. It was against the law to teach the Bible in anything but Latin, the official language of the church. How well he knew that.

The man's voice quivered with fear. 'How could they?' he snapped. 'It's as if it isn't our country at all.'

The man now leaned on the long, thick, oak table in the room for support. 'Vipers! Snakes! Foxes all of them!' he muttered angrily and spat at the fire.

Tyndale had often been tempted to call them worse, but he resisted saying so. Now was not the time. There was already enough anger and sadness in the room to go around.

'Would you be willing to pray with me?' Tyndale said. 'Our lives are in the hands of God.'

The man looked up from the top of his shoes. 'I'd like that,' he said sadly.

So Tyndale knelt down and began to pray loudly and confidently, even more bravely than he felt. 'Dear God, please help us in these terrible times,' he said. 'We don't understand all that is going on, but we know you do,' he continued. 'And we know you can help us, for doing the impossible is what you do better than anything else in the world. Please, Lord, we pray you would keep his friends safe at this time. Give him strength and keep him safe. Amen.' Now he looked again at the man, whose jaw was tight and unmoving and whose eyes, yellow with fear, still flitted almost constantly towards the door.

'I h-h-hesitated to come and tell you,' the man continued haltingly when Tyndale had finished praying, 'because I was afraid for my own life, but … you had to know. You, of all people, had to know.' The man's face turned back towards the fire, his hair – from the ride – remained unkempt and wild. He looked like a wild banshee on an English moor.

'We can't be afraid, friend,' said Tyndale confidently, more slowly and with a grave, unmistakable strength that seemed to build as he spoke. 'We cannot let fear win. We cannot be afraid. We must not be afraid, for God is with us.'

'And thank you,' he said, looking right into the man's eyes. 'It was kind of you to come to tell me – and very brave. I know it wasn't easy.'

There was a pause and the man even smiled.

'I really could only come when it got dark because – well, I have children too, you know,' he said, somehow looking a little more relaxed. 'Still, I should get going,' he said, raising his crumpled hood. Tyndale stepped forward to shake his hand.

'Thank you again, friend.'

'John,' the man said willingly and embraced him. 'The name's John.'

'Be careful,' Tyndale said.

'I will. You too,' he replied.

And with that, Tyndale stepped out of the door into the night air which was still dank, wet and cold from that afternoon's rain. The man slung one leg up to mount his horse, and horse and rider disappeared into the darkness, with only the rhythmical sound of the hooves breaking the silence. Not even the neighbour's dog howled tonight, and the owl which usually hooted from the willow tree just to assert his presence didn't make so much as a sound. Why were they so quiet? A sliver of moon winked from behind a large spreading oak, but even that was partially hidden by slowly moving clouds, slithering across its yellow face.

Tyndale spun quickly on his heels and headed back towards the house, his face a little white. He tried to shove his heart back down his throat; he had tried unsuccessfully to stuff it there at least three times tonight already. Granted, he had grown braver as the night wore on – this was God's work – but the chaotic speed at which things had happened earlier had left him a little cold and weary.

Now, heaving open the large, heavy, oak front door with both hands, he stepped back into Little Sodbury Manor.

When he entered, he found the Walsh children playing in one of the front rooms. As he wanted to be very careful not to scare them, Tyndale didn't say a word about anything that had happened. He simply smiled palely, exchanging full, uneasy glances with Sir John and Lady Anne and said flatly, 'I need to go to my room now. I have a few things to take care of.'

'Not now, Mr Tyndale, we want to play,' said the boy, tiptoeing past and laughing.

He smiled back. 'No, tomorrow we will play – and have lessons too,' he said.

'Yes, yes, of course,' Lady Anne said awkwardly, just trying to hold her own quivering voice steady in front of the children. 'Let Mr Tyndale get things done now.'

Tyndale trudged slowly back to his room. He was walking along the same corridor which twenty minutes ago he had run along in half the time. His mind and heart were still racing violently but his feet were tired and shuffling slowly. When he reached his room, he stoked the small fire, trying to urge a little dying orange-red light out of the embers. He picked the parchment up from the floor, placing it on his desk. It was a letter. Then he plopped down on the bed. He thought about writing to a friend, reading a book, riding wild boars into the sunset even though that wasn't something he did – anything, *anything*, he thought, but read the letter.

He looked over at it. He guessed who it might be from. But he didn't want to read it. Not now. Not ever.

'This is ridiculous,' he told himself. 'I can't not read it.'

Walking over to the desk, he finally forced himself to pick it up and read the address.

Sure enough it was from John Bell, Vicar-General of the diocese, the church authority in their area – Gloucestershire. He felt his stomach lurch.

Uncurling its edges, he forced himself to unscroll it and read. It said:

You are required to appear before His Excellency John Bell, local Vicar-General on the charge of heresy. Please appear next week at the ninth hour on the second day in the Year of our Lord 1522 to answer these charges.

John Bell,

Vicar-General.

Kings, Scholars and Vicars

Tyndale groaned and laid the letter down. John Bell had never been on Tyndale's list of favourite people and this letter didn't do anything to improve that fact. Still, he sighed. This was England in the 1500s. Tyndale knew his work was dangerous. It was simply a fact of life that anyone could be accused of heresy – of disagreeing with what the church in England taught – even when the church was wrong. The church could say one plus one equalled three and you were supposed to agree. The church could command you to sneeze and you were supposed to do it. But Tyndale didn't agree. They could never make him agree. They could threaten, torture or kill him but he was determined that the Bible should be translated into English. He would never say otherwise, no matter what they did to him. It should be translated and it should be read because it was God's holy Word and the people should be able to read it. It was just that simple.

He glanced down again at the black ink on the summons in front of him, which seemed hardly dry, and made his hands into fists, slamming one down on the table. 'No,' he hissed defiantly. 'NO.' Now he was practically shouting. 'So many of the priests don't even know Scripture,' he said, standing up defiantly. 'Many don't even know Latin. How can they teach the Bible in Latin if they don't know Latin? Besides, so many of them don't care about the people in their churches. They don't love them as Christ loves them. Some collect salaries and money from churches hundreds and hundreds of miles away.' He waved his arms as if he were shaking a sleeping person awake. 'Now, come off it! Who can't see through that? How can priests care for the people in their churches if they are hundreds of miles away? It is WRONG.'

He sat back down dolefully on the edge of the bed. 'Now, you're getting yourself all worked up again,' he told himself. 'Of course it's wrong.'

But it agitated him every time he thought of it; what they were doing was so unlike Christ, Tyndale sighed.

He crossed his feet, lay back on the bed and, watching the candle on the desk flicker uncertainly, thought back to being a child in Gloucestershire. Twenty years ago he could not have imagined his life now. Back then all you worried about was coming home late to dinner. Now you worried about coming home at all.

He stared out of the window into the black night sky. Beneath that murky, black sky lay the hills of Gloucestershire.

Gloucestershire had always been a beautiful place. The view from Stinchcombe Hill over the Vale of Berkeley where miles of trees and hedgerows ran in long green-brown patches had always been one of his favourites. He and his brother used to tease one another. 'And people still think the earth is flat, even though Christopher Columbus just proved it's round,' his brother would say.

Then they'd both look at the hills which stretched as far as the eye could see. 'I'm pretty sure anyone who thinks the earth is flat isn't from Gloucestershire,' he'd laugh back.

He glanced quickly down at the letter again.

Well, he could have seen this coming, sooner or later, in Gloucestershire or somewhere else.

As Tyndale lay on his bed and looked out at the stars, he thought about all the things that had brought him here, to this place at Little Sodbury. He thought about the letter that was sitting on his desk, calling him to answer for a charge of heresy. It was a funny thing, really. He wasn't that old, but sometimes his life seemed to be flying by. One minute he had been a small boy running around the hills of Gloucestershire, and the next he was a graduate of Oxford University and a priest, called to answer for a charge of heresy in the very area in which he had grown up. How did it all happen this fast anyway?

William Tyndale now traced the edge of the window thoughtfully with his finger and thought about his years there. Oxford had been quite a place, he knew. It had a reputation in England as an excellent university.

In particular he remembered the day he'd first arrived there. He remembered walking up the pathway and seeing the many spires along the horizon, reaching upwards towards the sky, like church steeples. At first he'd felt frightened and a little intimidated by the place. It seemed large. After all he was used to the open, green fields and lands of Gloucestershire.

Still, over his years at the university he'd learned to love the look of the spires on the horizon. He'd especially loved them in the evening, when the sun would wash them in a warm pink-gold and the whole world would seem richly beautiful and alive.

Then, too, there had been the library. How many hours had he put in, studying in the library? He felt like he'd known every bookshelf in the library, whether he wanted to or not.

The funny thing was, though, that it wasn't actually all the studying that had bothered him. Perhaps because he'd always been a good student he was used to that. What had bothered him during those years was all the courses he'd had to take before studying the Word of God. It had taken forever to get to the meat of God's Word in his studies there, and that had been frustrating. He was studying for a theology degree, after all. If you came to study God's Word at university, you should be able to do that and not have to study everything else first for years on end, as he did.

After graduating, he had gone to the city of Cambridge for some time.

Now Tyndale looked out at the bright pinprick of the stars in the velvet black. It was a very clear night. 'So,' he thought, 'it had come to this.' It was a funny feeling, knowing he had a Bachelor's degree and a Master's degree from this important university, and yet, for all that, he was being called to answer for a charge of heresy. Life took you in funny directions sometimes. He would never have guessed years ago that his life would have gone this way.

And yet … it wasn't a complete surprise to him.

Ever since he'd come to Little Sodbury Manor, he'd found himself disagreeing with the priests in the area. Sir John and Lady Anne Walsh had invited many of the clergy over to dine at the house, and he, William, had disagreed with so much of what they had said. So many of them didn't know the Scriptures well, and what they did know was often wrong. He had found it very frustrating.

William Tyndale now rolled over on his bed and looked back at the letter sitting on the desk. Finally, he got up to get ready to go to sleep. Tomorrow would come quickly, he knew.

He packed up the desk, tucked the letter under the edge of a stone paperweight, blew the candle out with a quick, hard puff and slumped noiselessly into bed; he finally fell asleep.

The following morning Tyndale woke to the smell of roasted pork, probably a few scraps from the night before, over the open fire. Maybe it was the smell of good food which finally roused him from sleep, but whatever it was, when he opened his eyes, he was glad to see that the giant face of Henry VIII, the King, bearing down on him with a sword, had only been part of a nightmare. He reminded himself that the smell of roasted meat was real. Good food always did something for you and this morning he needed something good.

Lady Anne approached him after breakfast. Sitting down at the table where he had almost finished eating, she began in a cautious voice. 'William, obviously there was a lot of activity here last night and in light of these events Sir John and I are very afraid for you. Can you tell me one more time – do you really have to go against the authorities? I know you've tried to tell me, but why is a translation in English so important?' she asked.

'*In principio creavit Deus caelum et terram*,' he answered, looking down and finishing the food on his plate.

'What?' she said, looking at him, puzzled.

'*In principio creavit Deus caelum et terram.*'

'William,' she said impatiently, 'that's Latin, isn't it? Now come off it! I'm trying to have a serious conversation with you.'

'I am having a serious conversation. Oh?' he said, feigning a look of innocence, 'so you would like me to speak to you in your own language. Hmmmm. Very interesting. I can't imagine why you would want that.'

'William – I know what you're getting at.'

'I am, Lady Anne, you are right. Try to remember that what you heard is exactly what the peasants hear every Sunday morning. Blah-blah-blah-blah. The priest might as well be saying "blitbledertanterwaldish" for all they understand.'

'Blitbleder-what?' said Lady Anne and laughed. She knew Tyndale had just made up a word to make his point.

'How can the peasants worship God in a language they don't understand? What does it matter what language?'

'Well, when you put it that way …' she said. 'Oh, I hate it when you are right,' she admitted. 'But they must know some of what is going on, don't you think, just from repetition? Maybe half?' she said tentatively, now not too sure of herself.

'Which half this week?'

'William …' she scolded.

'But it is true and there is so much the church adds or makes up, and the peasants don't know any of it because they can't read the Scriptures for themselves. What about purgatory, for instance?' he said insistently.

She sighed miserably. 'Somehow I thought you were going to say that.'

'Purgatory, or the idea that there is a middle place between heaven and hell,' Tyndale explained, 'is not in the Bible. It doesn't exist and yet the church demands money from people to get themselves and their friends out of it.' He shuddered as if he had seen a ghost. 'How can we stand by and let the church of God teach that you can BUY God's goodness?' If the teaching of purgatory had been a bowl of soup, one had the definite idea Tyndale would have spat it out.

Lady Anne's face grimaced sympathetically. 'Well, yes, I admit there may be things not taught in the Bible exactly, but remember, England sells those "indulgences" or promises to get people out of purgatory less than other countries do.'

'But they still sell them – and they are still wrong,' he said, gritting his teeth together.

'Ah, this is painful for you, William. I can see that. But can't we change things slowly? Do we really need to change everything at once?' she asked.

He winced. 'We need to teach people the truth as soon as possible. No time is too early to correct wrong in the teaching of God's Word, for the church of God can't go forward until people can see for themselves in God's Word that these doctrines are not right. And the only way they can see that is if they can read them to see for themselves. I want everyone to know that Christ paid for all our sins on the cross and we don't need to pay for any of them. Don't you?'

'Oh, William.' This time Lady Anne threw her hands up in the air. 'You win. You win. You're right. I can't argue with you when you're right, especially about Christ's work for us. And you are right.' She spun around to say something to the cook who was now beginning to baste lamb, chop cabbage and add leeks and onions to cook for dinner. The cook wiped her hands, spattering fat. 'Still,' Lady Anne said when she turned back to speak to William once more, 'please be careful with guests at my house. It's a little delicate, as you know, for Sir John and I are known in this area.'

'For your sake and your husband's, I'll try. I do try and I will keep trying, even though it is hard.'

Lady Anne laughed. 'I know, William. You are intelligent and educated and that makes it harder for you. You can see when things are translated or taught in a wrong way. Still, many other scholars are bright and sharp as well. Do you really think all the opinions of so many bright, educated men are wrong?'

'If you could read these things for yourself, you might see it is not my opinion but God's opinion in his Word. Speaking of which, you should read Erasmus' book *A Manual for a Christian Soldier*, for instance. It's a good book to demonstrate the idea that Christianity should reach to the everyday man – makes great bedtime reading and really might convince you.'

'It's not in English ...'

'Well, it wasn't, but it is now. I have translated it for you and Sir John to read.'

Lady Anne looked surprised. 'Well, William,' she said more patiently, 'Erasmus is not illegal. I will read him and form my own opinion. But –' She stopped and looked down awkwardly. 'But you are a step beyond Erasmus in some of the things you say and believing it is Christ alone who saves people. Many, many have burned at the stake for your beliefs. If you are right ...' She couldn't finish that sentence. She wouldn't think about that right now.

The week proved uneventful, but the following week, the morning of Tyndale's meeting with John Bell dawned unusually bright and cold; a chill wind whipped its way around the valley, slapping at loose clothes, stealing hats, undoing people's hair and otherwise causing mischief all over Gloucestershire. Tyndale rose early, got dressed and left the house promptly, to make it on time. Still, when he finally clapped the door of Little Sodbury Manor shut behind him, he found himself walking very slowly towards the church at which he was to meet John Bell. If you walked slowly, you could convince yourself this wasn't really happening to you.

When he arrived, a grey-haired man ushered him into the great hall of the church, pointing him to a dark, carved oak chair in a large room. It was cold and draughty where he sat. Long white candles burned at one end of the room and a high, ornate ceiling hung over his head, with gold overlay running up every wall and ceiling vault, much, he thought, like the gilded bars on a very fancy cage.

'Mr Tyndale,' the archdeacon said stiffly and authoritatively when he entered, his eyes barely glancing at Tyndale. 'The priests in my diocese tell me you are troublesome. You disagree with them, you argue, you agitate. I don't like agitators.' He leaned menacingly towards Tyndale, overemphasising every word. William was sure the hairs on the back of his neck were on fire. 'They tell me,' the archdeacon continued in a low, acrid voice, 'that you do not give them respect.' His breath was now warm on Tyndale's neck and far, far too close.

'I respect all who teach the Word of God truly,' Tyndale retorted without flinching.

'Am I to understand,' the archdeacon continued archly, 'that you think the Bible should be for the common man? Is this true?' he said, sweeping his hands in the air as if he were in a giant parade.

Tyndale still did not move. He looked around at the church. He was unimpressed by show without heart. His response was respectful but earnest. 'The Word of God should be for the common man,' he insisted. 'We need more of the Word of God.'

At this the choir-boy attending in the room tried to hide a smirk behind his hand, but the archdeacon's face grew taut and angry, and his lips very, very thin. 'You know, don't you, Mr Tyndale, that translating the Scriptures into English is against the law?' he said acidly.

Tyndale paused and answered slowly this time.

'I do ... But don't you see? – the church has added so many things,' Tyndale answered. 'Indulgences, saints, images – all clutter and junk. People simply can't see what is true because of all the rubbish that has got in the way. They can't see Christ.'

'To see Christ, Mr Tyndale,' the Vicar-General hissed back, 'all persons need the church. Like small children, we are their eyes. Asking the peasants to understand the Word of God is like trying to teach doctoring to small children. Children can't know what a doctor knows any more than an ox could, and no one should ask them to. Would you tell children to learn surgery? Or maybe the ox should learn it?' Here he laughed a high, cold, cruel laugh. Tyndale resisted the urge to tell him the joke wasn't even funny.

'*Pater noster qui in caelis es, sanctificetur nomen tuum,*' Tyndale answered, looking directly into John Bell's eyes. 'When the people hear that in Latin, nobody knows what it means – and you know that. You know they don't know they are saying, 'Our Father which art in heaven, may thy name be sanctified.' For all they know, they might be saying, 'The ox is eating the purple grass.' It cannot help them worship if they don't understand it.'

The archdeacon looked at Tyndale contemptuously. He didn't like having his cow picture given back to him. He frowned maliciously and spoke in a grating voice. 'Watch your tone with me, Mr Tyndale.'

'Yes, Your Grace,' Tyndale answered as humbly as he could bear. 'But it is true. People should know they are speaking of the wonder and majesty of God,' he persisted. Why he was even trying to explain it to this man he wasn't sure. He wasn't getting anywhere.

Once again John Bell's face grew taut and grave, and his brows knit sharply. Finally he said darkly, 'This meeting is over, Mr Tyndale. I have heard enough for one day. But watch yourself – or one day the shadow of the church may fall long on you.' He smiled and yellow crooked teeth showed through. Tyndale shivered and recoiled as if he'd been bitten by a snake. His mouth was dry.

'It's cold in here,' was all he said as he stood to leave.

He nodded and left. Part of him was glad the meeting was over, for he knew it would do no good to plead the truth any more with this man. No words he could say here would make a difference. Talking sense to John Bell about this was like trying to move the sea.

Besides, Tyndale took the warnings of the archdeacon seriously. 'The shadow of the church,' he thought, as the church door clapped shut behind him. 'I don't really like the sound of that.' His stomach was a little queasy.

As he made his way back to the large manor house he wrestled with what he should do. Obviously John Bell was not someone to change his mind. He was stubborn, foolish even. Tyndale had to ask himself: Was he putting Sir John and Lady Anne Walsh at risk by staying with them and would his disagreement with the authorities in Gloucestershire put everyone in the house in danger? He thought about the faces of the children he had grown to love and shuddered – would they be in danger also? And then what about the work? What about the translation? He certainly couldn't continue to do it here, for things were getting dangerous. What should he do?

'Ah, William, William ...' Sir John greeted him warmly at the door and grabbed his arm, his eyes narrowing with intense interest and curiosity. 'What did he say?'

'Ah, Sir John. It was what we expected. No more, no less.' Tyndale poked at a loose stone with his toe, his eyes downcast.

'That's a no, then. But what are you going to do?' Sir John asked, looking a little uncertain. Tyndale surprised even himself when the words came out of his mouth. 'I will do God's work,' he said with determination, 'even if they try to kill me between my translating the words "God" and "created heaven and earth".'

Sir John stared at Tyndale. Courage like this was very rare.

'Good for you,' he said quietly before asking the important question, 'And how will you do this?' Sir John continued, 'Even if you do translate it, no one in England will print it since printing it is still illegal.'

'Well,' Tyndale said sensibly, 'I will pack my bags and go to London for help. My plan is to hunt down the Bishop of London if he will see me and try to get his approval for my work. People have told me his mind is more open than that of other clergy – like John Bell – ' he muttered disgustedly, 'though he is still part of the church. If I could get approval from the bishop,' he said brightly, 'then it wouldn't be illegal any more. You know … maybe this is God's way of making it possible.'

'Ah, William. Your persistence and commitment amaze me. Well, so be it. If you really do decide to go, my wife has a cousin there who will let you stay with him until you can find a place to stay long-term, or decide what to do.'

Tyndale was very grateful. 'Thank you, Sir John – my mind is made up,' he said. 'And – ' he paused a little awkwardly, 'thank you. Living with you and your family these past years has been a joy – really.' He grabbed Sir John's hand and shook it vigorously.

Sir John looked directly into William's face before adding, 'It is a fact, William, that over the time that you have been with us, tutoring our children and living in our home, both Lady Anne and myself have become more and more convinced of the truth and importance of the things that you stand for and teach.'

William bowed before Sir John, smiling, thankful, his heart full of joy.

And as his employer turned to go back into the house, he placed his arm on his young employee's shoulder. 'And remember the offer of hospitality with my wife's cousin, Poyntz. She will be glad to have you stay, which means you will be able to preach at St Dunstan's again. That sounds like a good plan.'

Tyndale smiled. He'd have accommodation and a place to preach – his needs would be cared for and he would be among some old friends too.

Finally Tyndale was ready to set off for London. As he said goodbye to the Walsh family, he felt the pang of what was sure to be a long separation from them. Goodbyes had a nasty sting. 'Still,' he reminded himself, 'the prospect of meeting with the bishop is exciting. Perhaps it is time.'

The summer grass danced around the wagon wheels in a light, easy breeze. He'd miss the deep autumnal colours which would be falling here at Little Sodbury, then winter's beautiful white blanket on the old manor house.

The English countryside passed before him. There were long stretches of grey-green fields and sheep grazing peacefully. The evening sun was beginning to wane from a fiery yellow to a late-day mellow gold.

As the wagon-carriage underneath him rattled along, Tyndale noticed a man and a young boy ploughing in one of the fields. The man was clearly getting old, too old to be doing this kind of back-breaking work. He mopped the sweat from his forehead with a thick cloth and then tried to rub a little life into his hard, brown, stiff hands. When Tyndale saw it, he felt sorry for the man, and he could not help thinking back to what he himself had said to a clergyman once.

He remembered the conversation as if it were yesterday. He'd been discussing, even arguing, with a local clergyman. Tyndale smiled – it happened often now – it was nothing unusual. But, peeved at the disagreement, the clergyman had hissed angrily at Tyndale, 'We had better be without God's law than the Pope's.'

William had felt stunned. Could he really be saying that the Pope was more important than God? How could anyone believe that any law or word was more important than God's? What a terrible, unthinkable thing to say.

'If God chooses to spare my life,' he had shot back instantly, 'after many years I will cause a boy who drives the plough to know more of the Scriptures than you do.'

Even now, as the wagon bumped steadily along, crunching on every clump in the road, Tyndale looked back at the two ploughmen working hard in the fields. He said firmly in as quiet a voice as possible, 'Lord willing, we will get the Word of God where it belongs – into your hands.'

'So, what do you think of these Reformers, eh?'

The man driving the wagon, a thin slight man, was making conversation. He probably heard Tyndale talking to himself and wanted to size him up. 'Don't know much of this man, Martin Luther, but he sure shook things up in Germany, didn't he?'

Tyndale laughed. 'That he did.'

'What was all the fuss about, anyhow? An awful lot of smoke over a little piece of paper, eh?'

The man knew little of Tyndale except that he had been to Oxford, had studied religion and theology there, and was now an ordained priest. Tyndale laughed again. The driver's comment was the understatement of a lifetime, but he did not want to hurt the man's feelings.

'What are you laughing about, anyway?' the man said.

'I was laughing because it wasn't exactly just a piece of paper,' Tyndale said, still laughing.

'Well, what was it then?'

'Luther believed things different from the church and hung the paper as a direct challenge to some of those things,' Tyndale answered. 'It's not the paper but what was on the paper. There were some pretty important things on that paper.'

'Well, I don't know about all that. I goes to church like everyone else. Some of those church fellows are a bit big for their breeches, what with taking money from those who can't afford it. Tried to buy my mother out of purgatory last year but I couldn't pay for it. I have to feed my family, you know. I try to pray to God to get her out but the church tells me it don't work that way.'

'It is only the grace of Christ that keeps us from the anger of God, my friend,' Tyndale said.

'Boy, I hope you're right. I'd rather trust in Christ than those priests any day! You seem to know what you're talking about. But hey, I see we are almost there.'

'Yes, my friend. Thank you for your trouble. And catch every word you can of the Word of God. Leave nothing out and add nothing to it. Pray to Christ and him alone.'

The man looked around, 'You really think I don't have to buy her out?' he said in wonder. 'What a great thought.' He looked up. 'God speed to you, sir.'

'And to you,' Tyndale said, shaking his hand.

The Big Meeting

The following morning dawned full of light misty drizzle. When Tyndale rolled out of bed at the Poyntz' house, he rubbed his eyes, yawned widely and slapped cold water on his face, trying to blink out a short night of sleep. He may not have slept well but he was glad to be staying with Lady Anne's relatives … even though the accommodation here wasn't up to the same standards as Little Sodbury. But though these people were being very generous to him, William hoped that he wouldn't have to impose on them too much longer. They had little enough space as it was.

Opening the small wooden shutters, he looked out onto the streets of the busy capital. London's city streets were already bustling. The home of the palace, the hub of England, a centre for trade and education, London's streets drew action like a magnet. People crossed and re-crossed streets, rushing around to get to work and finish business. The common people tramped dutifully along in plain clothes, woollen tights and black, buckled shoes. Elsewhere, gentlemen strolled leisurely by in elegant clothes, some in very fancy breeches – short breech-like trousers – beautifully striped. A horse cart rattled by.

So … this was it – the big morning. An employment interview, a test of nerves; it seemed to Tyndale like a dream.

Tyndale quickly got dressed and left the house. As he began his journey he cast his eye over some of the great white stone buildings of the city and watched the steady grey rain stream down from the sky. Gradually he played back in his mind the words of a good friend of his, who had spoken to him before he had left Gloucestershire.

'Be careful, William,' his friend had said. 'In your excitement, don't forget – the church has eyes and ears everywhere. The bishop is open-minded but he is still part of the church, and the church is dangerous to you now. Don't anger him. Think about your words before you speak them.'

'Yes, yes, I know,' he had said. 'Remember – it is in God's hands.'

Still, as he plodded along now, he went over in his mind what he would say and how he would say it. 'Bishop Tunstall, Your Grace …' No, he didn't have to say both. That was redundant. 'Bishop Tunstall, I am honoured that you would see me …' No, that was a little bit like begging. He wanted to appear dignified. 'Oh, stop,' he finally told himself. 'It's in the Lord's hands. You know that. You know what you need to say.'

He finally reached the front door of the church, a church much larger than the one in Gloucestershire, and he knocked on the beautiful, wooden door.

When a polite grey-haired man let him in, Tyndale felt dwarfed under the huge canopy of the cathedral ceiling. Paintings graced the walls. Everything inside the church stretched the eye upwards. Long, narrow windows accompanied a ceiling that went so high he couldn't imagine anyone, even without fear of heights, fixing or painting it.

He was led by an altar boy to the room in which the bishop worked.

'Come in, Mr Tyndale, come in,' a moderate voice said from inside. It was the bishop. Tyndale felt nervous, his mouth dry, his skin clammy.

He entered.

'Now,' said the bishop, sitting behind a large wooden table, his long bishop's cap extending up from the top of his head. 'You asked to meet with me. What can I do for you?' His voice was even and low.

'Uh – uh,' Tyndale stammered. 'Thank you, Your Grace, for seeing me.' He recovered quickly. 'I have heard many good things of your being a bishop here in London.' Tyndale tried not to sound like he was flattering the man, but the bishop was honestly known as a moderate, educated man, polite and well-spoken – that was true. And Tyndale desperately wanted to make a good impression. A lot depended on this moment.

'I serve by the Lord's grace here,' the bishop said. 'Now, exactly what can I do for you?'

'Well,' Tyndale's palms were sweating freely, but he held them close together so the bishop couldn't see that. 'I am seeking work here in London and wondered whether you would consider hiring me.'

'Hmmmmm.' The bishop looked thoughtful. 'And what kind of work would you like to do that you want to be in London and to work in my house?'

Now Tyndale bit hard on the inside of his mouth. 'Please, Lord,' he prayed silently. 'I want to translate the Scriptures, Your Grace,' he said.

'But the Scriptures have been translated,' the bishop replied, meeting Tyndale's eyes with a wrinkly, puzzled expression.

'Into English,' Tyndale said, knowing his words would land heavy and hard on the bishop's ears. The bishop blinked a few times.

Tyndale continued, 'I studied languages well and can show good work in a number of them.' He paused, gripping the chair underneath him, his knuckles turning white. 'I see a need for translation of the Scriptures to English from the original languages.'

Tyndale wasn't sure he had breathed once the whole time. He wondered how he would be seen or understood. Being a moderate man, the bishop probably wouldn't kill him at the stake, but news could circulate and there were plenty of people who would. Still, Tyndale wasn't sure at that moment if it would be worse to be killed or to be told no. Being told no wouldn't simply disappoint – it would break his heart. Moments passed quietly, no sound passing between the two men until …

'Yes, yes, I can see you do have an ability to work with languages. The oration of Isocrates which my assistant Harry Guildford has brought me, your translation from Greek to English, appears to be very well done.'

'Thank you, Your Grace,' Tyndale's heart rose hopefully.

Then there was a pause. The bishop shuffled a few papers on his desk and rose.

'But,' he said walking to the window, 'I should tell you, Mr Tyndale, that my house doesn't need anyone at this time. Still, don't worry,' he added. 'I'm certain an educated man like yourself will have no trouble finding work here in the city.' He finished this last sentence brightly, his eyes lighting up reassuringly as he turned back towards Tyndale.

Tyndale's heart fell. He knew this was Tunstall's way of saying 'no', not just to him, but to the work. He tried not to show by his face that he was crestfallen. 'But, Your Grace,' he said one last time, knowing this last attempt was probably futile, 'you are one of the few bishops who has the mind of a scholar and the position to make it possible.'

'There is just no room,' Tunstall repeated quietly, his long robes brushing against themselves as he walked.

In that one stark horrible moment Tyndale knew translating the Bible into English in England would not happen. He stared out at the rain.

'Are you quite well, Mr Tyndale?' the bishop said, now leaning over him, looking concerned.

'Oh, yes, I am fine, Your Grace,' he said blankly, but as he left he did not feel well at all. His stomach felt knotted and hard, his head dizzy, his heart broken.

Just then, the altar boy came to collect him and show him the way to the front door.

'Thank you,' Tyndale said grimly and pushed open the door.

He still couldn't believe it. The church had refused him. They had turned him away. He wanted to bellow back at the gargoyles on either side of the front door or knock them right off their snooty stone perches. But what good would that do? The worst part was knowing 'no' in London meant NO in all England. Bishop Tunstall was the most open-minded of all the bishops in the country. And without the support of a bishop the work remained illegal. NO was now final. That was the part he simply couldn't accept.

Tyndale went back to his lodgings and put his head in his hands. His heart sagged miserably. Now that the printing press had made the copying of books easier, it had seemed like such a good opportunity to get a translation into the hands of the people, a good translation, an errorless translation, a translation in *English*. He felt called by God to do it. Would God let the work die? He sat in his lodgings and looked out of the window at the city, musing on the fact that the forces at work here were clearly larger than he was. The church appeared to be too strong for him – there was nothing he could do.

He was thankful when his heavy thoughts were interrupted by a knock at his bedroom door. A small, young voice said, 'Father asked me to remind you, sir, that church is tomorrow and you are scheduled to preach at St Dunstan's. He asked me to make sure you are up to it. Are you ill, Mr Tyndale?'

'No,' said Tyndale. 'I'm not ill, just sick at heart, but never mind. And as you have reminded me that tomorrow is God's day I feel much better,' he now said brightly. 'We'll be in God's house on God's day. Doesn't that seem right?' He grinned, wanting Poyntz's son to see only the joy of what it means to be part of God's world. His heart, though, still ached. He couldn't bring himself to tell a child that men were standing in the way of God. Maybe it was time to quit, to realise that he had tried and failed. Maybe he was pushing too hard. Maybe it wasn't time.

But the moment he thought this, he knew it was wrong. Tyndale thought back to the joy he had of seeing people read for the very first time. He couldn't imagine what it must be like to put an English Bible into a person's hands for the first time – God's very Word, to read. He remembered the young ploughboy and the rough hands of the old man in the field. All of a sudden he remembered – oh no, he had a lunch appointment to discuss his plans. If he didn't hurry up, he would be late.

'Maybe God is telling us it is not yet the time,' the friend said, after Tyndale had finished his story about Tunstall, putting down his pewter mug.

'No, it has been the time,' Tyndale protested. 'The time has come and gone a hundred times. The fruit was ripe a hundred years ago – it smells like rotting cabbage, it is so overripe. England could go on for hundreds of years this way – it already has. John Wycliffe tried to do this within the last hundred and fifty years and England is no better for his work, because it wasn't printed and therefore it cannot reach most, perhaps any of them. The ordinary peasant is still unable to read God's Word in his own language. Besides, it is not just anyone who can translate well. It needs to be a very good scholar who knows the language well and will not be lazy about God's Word. When will the next scholar be raised up by God?'

'God can raise up men,' the friend replied.

'Yes, I agree,' he answered, 'but how many ploughmen will die without Christ before England stops saying 'no'? Think about it. We can't let hundreds die without Christ because they don't know the truth. We need the Word *now*.'

The friend nodded sadly. 'I agree with you, William, I really do. I just don't know what to tell you to do.'

'I know I need to find a way – England needs the Word.' It was what Tyndale felt. It was also what he knew. He would not quit. He could not.

In spite of his frustration, the following morning Tyndale preached at St Dunstan's. Halfway through the morning, the sun, thankfully, broke through the dull, grey mist, catapulting beams of light through the church windows. It burst in on the people of God, flooding the pews, bouncing off the dull, brown walls. Tyndale preached that morning on the mercy of God. Preaching about God's mercy and love always brought something to life inside him again. He felt comforted.

He looked out over the congregation. There they were, many of the people he knew so well. There was Mr Kitktz, the crusty old man who lived a block from the church. And Dorothy and John Wollop, with the six children, like little geese, behind them. And Harvey and Hollister Fieldstone, field hands, a little grimy for church maybe, but welcome all the same. The people and the Word of God. He just couldn't think of a better combination.

After the service Tyndale stood at the back door and greeted the people from the church, shaking each hand vigorously as they left.

'We appreciated your preaching, Mr Tyndale,' an elderly woman with a thick black cane said. He shook her hand a little more delicately, for she was a little frail.

'Come and preach again some time,' said a man in a broad velvety hat.

'Nice to have you with us today,' a young woman and her husband affirmed.

One man, however, in a beautiful, rich, silk cloth coat was especially anxious to meet him. 'Humphrey Monmouth's the name,' the broad-shouldered man said warmly. 'I live about three miles away and have come before when you preached at St Dunstan's. We appreciate what you have to say from God's Word.' His eyes shone with respect.

'Thank you. It is a pleasure to meet you,' Tyndale said sincerely, nodding.

'I do wish I could talk longer,' Monmouth continued, 'You seem like the kind of fellow worth having a conversation with, but I must admit I'm in a mad dash today. Wife has the fever – you know the drill. Maybe some other time.'

'Yes, I'd like that,' Tyndale said.

As that was the sum total of the conversation with Humphrey Monmouth for now, Tyndale didn't think any more about it. It was simply a brief handshake, a word or two of conversation, fancy, striking clothes and an appreciative comment, nothing more.

That afternoon Tyndale ate lunch at home with the Poyntzes. With thick brown bread and golden butter, roasted duck and parsnips for lunch, a man could get fat eating here, Tyndale thought.

'This is a wonderful meal, Mrs Poyntz,' he said. 'There is never a lack of food or love in this house.'

'Man shall not live by bread only,' she said humbly and sincerely. 'I'm glad you enjoyed it, but it is your sermon which fed our souls.'

'Ah, but thankfully we won't have to run your sermon off,' exclaimed Mr Poyntz, laughing and patting his stomach.

'Thomas,' said his wife and shook her head, laughing. 'He's incorrigible.'

Tyndale laughed too.

The following week Tyndale had an errand to run in town. As he rushed down the street he almost toppled a man coming the other way.

'Sorry,' said Tyndale apologetically. 'Apparently I wasn't paying attention.'

'Apparently,' said the man brusquely, brushing himself off.

Tyndale apologetically collected his papers from the ground and looked up, following the fancy gold medallion around the man's neck glinting brightly in the sun – up to the man's face.

'Hey, wait,' the man said as Tyndale looked up. 'I know you from somewhere.' He scratched his head.

Tyndale thought the broad hat and rich, dark clothes did look vaguely familiar.

'Wait – I know – Tyndale. William Tyndale,' the man exclaimed as he finally recognised him and placed him. 'Ha! Who would have thought a good man like you would be running people over in the streets?' It was Humphrey Monmouth.

'Sorry,' said Tyndale, looking at his feet. 'It was an accident – really.'

'Sir Humphrey Monmouth,' the man now said, breaking into a wide smile and extending his hand. 'I don't know if you remember me.'

'Oh yes,' Tyndale recalled. 'On a Sunday – at St Dunstan's.' He paused. 'Yes. You did seem like a good man, certainly not the kind I should be running over in the streets.'

'No, you shouldn't,' Monmouth repeated, laughing.

Henry Monmouth smiled warmly and straightened his hat. 'You will probably recall I didn't have much time that Sunday to talk to you, as my wife was not feeling great.'

'Yes, I remember, and of course I understand,' Tyndale said sympathetically.

'But I hope I made clear that we enjoyed your preaching very much.'

'Thank you, sir. I am always glad the Lord gives me the opportunity to do it.' Tyndale nodded.

'So, what about you? What are you doing these days?' Monmouth now pressed with interest.

'Well,' said Tyndale slowly, 'I moved here wanting to do work in London.' He shifted his feet. 'I went to Bishop Tunstall to do it, but he tells me his house is full.'

'Ah,' said Humphrey Monmouth thoughtfully, his eyes lighting up. 'If you are looking for a place to stay in order to do your work, what about my house? It's a monstrously sized place – probably could fit an elephant in one of the back bedrooms – there is plenty of room. We'd be happy to have you.'

Tyndale looked surprised. 'Are you serious? I was looking for a place. The Poyntzes have been great but their house is not large. I am afraid I am sometimes in the way.'

'Of course I am serious.' Humphrey Monmouth looked confident. 'It's settled then.'

That night, Tyndale told the Poyntzes, who were very glad for him that he had found a house he could live in long-term. He packed his bags and within the week had moved into the house of Humphrey Monmouth, wealthy cloth merchant.

It was a large place, and as Monmouth claimed had plenty of room. God seemed somehow to always provide.

Tyndale spent endless hours there, in the back rooms leaning over the Scriptures, working. His eyes strained, his back hurt, but he would never complain. He was very glad to be doing the work – it was all the reward he needed. He worked hard, often taking walks as breaks now and then throughout the city, but trying hard not to run over anyone else.

Still, the conversation he had most during that time was the one he had with himself and God. 'How? How can I get a translation into English when it is declared illegal by the King? No printer will print it.'

One bright morning, not long after his move to Monmouth's house, Tyndale set out on an errand to town to pick up a few things. As he was walking along one of the town streets, thinking what a nice morning it was and working on the word for a particular passage in his mind, he happened to see a man rummaging through a crate. 'Awfully ratty packing for an imported glazed plate,' he heard the man mutter, holding the plate up to the light and inspecting it for cracks. 'People should be more careful when they pack these things,' he growled.

Tyndale stopped, frozen in his tracks. 'More careful when they pack these things,' he thought. 'Wait a minute …'

He seemed rooted to the spot. Raising his head, he stared at the man, almost gawking.

'Never seen a plate before, mister?' the man said, annoyed, but Tyndale looked right at him. 'Sorry,' he said quickly. 'It caught the sun and … well, never mind, I must be going.'

But it was all he could do not to whoop out loud, right there in the street. 'That's it,' he said to himself, as he walked quickly away. That was it. Why had he never thought of it before? Cornmeal came into London from other countries. So did rye and wheat, tar, flax and hemp. Even books like Luther's came into England smuggled in barrels or sacks with legal goods. Why not? Why not God's Word?

The young scholar wanted to throw his hands up in the air and sing a hymn. He wanted to run, shout, dance. He wanted to celebrate and throw a feast. That was it. He put his hand to his forehead. Yes, yes, that was it. He would go to the continent and do his work there. There were more printers there and he stood a better chance of getting it printed!

Reaching the edge of the street, he ran all the way home. Full-grown men didn't normally run, but he was too excited – he couldn't simply walk. And, in fact, it was ironic, really. For if someone on the street that day had seen this scholar half-walking, half-running home, they would never have guessed what he was up to. No one – not even the dumpy, friendly-looking man holding the plate and still staring down the street at him – would ever have guessed that this man, William Tyndale, was half out of his mind over an idea that could mean he would be hunted and chased down like an animal or even killed. Who would have guessed that he had formed a plan which could easily cost him his life? He was just an ordinary man walking along an ordinary street, but William Tyndale believed in a God who was anything but ordinary. William could see clearly what needed to be done and he knew this plan was a good one.

'Someone is here to see you, William,' Humphrey said, when Tyndale blustered through the front door at Monmouth's house.

'Who is it?' Tyndale asked, smoothing his hair and trying to get his excitement under control.

'John, John Frith,' the servant said. 'He's in the guest room.'

'Thank you,' Tyndale said. This was too good to be true, he thought.

'John, John Frith!' He said when he saw his friend

They had met in London and talked before about the need for a translation of the Bible into English, and Tyndale was excited to see him again.

'William, you look almost crazed,' John said when Tyndale entered the room. 'What? What is it?'

'John, I've got it. The Lord just gave me the idea. I know what I am going to do.'

'What?' John said, bewildered.

'Crates, barrels and boxes. I'm going to the continent. I'm going to send my books to England the same way Luther's books have come. What's a little English law to stop God? Ha!' He gestured wildly, ran around in a few circles and finally collapsed, laughing, into a heap on the floor. He whooped one last time then tried to catch his breath.

'So? So?' he said. 'What do you think?'

John Frith looked on in wonder. 'You are mad, Mr Tyndale.' He paused, reflecting slowly. 'Are you sure you have thought this through? It could be dangerous.'

'John,' Tyndale exclaimed, 'translating the Bible has always been dangerous! Of course it is dangerous to do God's work!'

'Point well taken,' John admitted, smiling. 'Well, it does have real possibilities ...' he said.

'Possibilities? John, on the continent, Bible translating is not illegal. It's my only chance to do the work God has called me to. I know which way the tide of opinion is going here – but it's time to go against the tide ...'

'You're right, William. I know you are right,' John said with growing excitement.

The following morning, Tyndale mentioned to Monmouth that he would soon be moving to the continent.

'Really?' said Monmouth. 'Well … allow me to give you some money before you go. I can even give you a few hints about travel in continental Europe, I have done so much of it myself.' Monmouth went on, 'Your life in my house has been godly and above reproach these six months. You have lived as a good priest should and have not spent your days in a lazy fashion. You are a hard worker. I wish you well, William, I really do.'

'Thank you, Humphrey. You have been more than generous in taking me in. If I never see you again here on earth, thank you for all your kindness.'

'Now stop it, William, don't even – don't you dare talk like that. You are going to the continent now, where things are freer.'

But Humphrey knew, in spite of what he said, that William Tyndale had not chosen a safe life.

One morning, not long after, Humphrey Monmouth left for a business trip and William Tyndale left for a place far away, to begin a new life outside England, the only place he had ever known. The continent – the rest of Europe outside England – was somewhere beyond the horizon and it waited for him.

A Changing World

The large boat which Tyndale boarded now began to travel down the River Thames. The city of London grew smaller behind him, until it was finally lost from sight. Soon they reached the mouth of the river, then the open sea. As the cool breezes washed over Tyndale's face, England itself began to grow smaller. The boat swayed, as it rose and fell against the white-capped water, underneath a sharp blue sky.

Tyndale thought to himself about where he might go, once the boat reached shore. There were lots of places to try.

'Good morning.' An elderly man with a well-trimmed beard and deep hazel eyes wandered up to him on the boat and began to chat.

'Good morning,' Tyndale replied.

'Gorgeous, isn't it?'

'Beautiful.'

'So, where are you off to on this beautiful morning?'

'Germany,' Tyndale said flatly, trying not to be rude but also trying not to show any interest. No one knew anything about him just yet, but he wanted to learn to keep from saying much. He wasn't anxious to have this conversation, for he was afraid he might say something he needed to keep a secret.

'Whereabouts in Germany?' the man continued eagerly.

Where in Germany? 'Oh dear,' Tyndale thought and could feel himself freeze. He couldn't answer that question out loud, for details would be far too dangerous. The details weren't dangerous to him yet – the people around him didn't yet know what he was going to do – but he did – and he wanted to get into the habit of giving up as little information as possible. In fact, he didn't even know the answer himself. 'Oh, lots of places,' he said, which wasn't exactly untrue. He would, after all, be travelling. But the difference would be that he was a man on the run, without a country, a nomad, a wanderer for God. William would be hiding in alleyways and sneaking around corners, living by trust in God … there weren't many other travellers who could claim that.

'How about you?' William asked the gentleman. He wanted to try and get the focus off himself.

'Oh, I'm going home after a lot of tiring business. I live in Brussels,' the man said, smiling widely.

'Oh,' Tyndale returned the smile, but tried now to move closer to the side of the ship. Fortunately the man took the hint. 'Oh well, nice meeting you,' he said in a friendly manner and slunk off.

'I hope I didn't look rude,' Tyndale thought. 'But no one must know exactly where I am going,' he reminded himself.

Tyndale now stood at the edge of the ship, watching the clouds float through the endless blue sky and tried to figure out where he was going to live.

'A French city? Paris, Lyon maybe? No ...' he ruled France out because most of it remained far too Catholic. 'Much of France believes things which are very similar to what I just left,' he thought. 'Spain? What about Spain? No, same story. The Low Countries? Ah, now the Low Countries has some possibilities. An excellent trade route, and a number of areas in the Low Countries believe exactly as I do.'

Still, as he tossed options around in his mind, turning them over and over again, he felt Germany, with its strong love for the ideas to which he had committed his life, made the most sense. Germany had demonstrated over and over again in recent years that it believed strongly in reform, in changing wrong ideas to make them truer to the Bible. In addition, Germany boasted an extremely strong printing press. Many of the Christian believers in that country believed in salvation by faith, not works. And this, Tyndale knew, was the most important doctrine in the world.

Of course, Tyndale knew no place was entirely safe – people travelled, and gossip happened everywhere. Whispers in taverns, chit-chat and wagging tongues over dinner couldn't be stopped. You could be unsafe in any country. Still, Germany looked like a pretty good spot to take his first chance. Germany it would be.

He breathed a sigh of relief.

'Now – on to the task of picking a city,' he thought. Well, this wasn't quite as difficult. There were plenty of attractive cities – Hamburg, Cologne, Marburg,

Wittenburg ... but he felt it would be easier to decide when he got there, based on who had a willing printer.

Finally the boat docked at shore. It pulled up to the land and shiphands threw ropes to secure it. The ship's great swaying bow which had once rollicked hard on the open sea now stopped and swayed only gently. With other passengers, Tyndale made his way down the plank and took his first step onto continental Europe. The sky which looked down on him was a deep, vibrant blue, and the sun now blazed out from behind some billowing white clouds. He took a deep breath. His face flushed with anticipation.

Hoisting his weatherbeaten trunk under one arm, he now began to walk away from the boat. There was a lot to get organised. It was time to begin the business of finding a place to stay and a printer. However, he hadn't gone far when he happened to find himself just behind an old man and a young boy. They were having a very interesting conversation about Germany. Though Tyndale was too polite to intentionally eavesdrop, he was going in that direction already and it was simply hard not to overhear.

'Whew!' said the old man, who had grey bushy hair and an old, wrinkly and weatherbeaten face. 'I am glad we have arrived safely, grandson. Our crossing was favourable, God be thanked. Though we have had a safe journey so far we must be careful – the world is not the place it once was. Travellers like us have to be careful ...'

Tyndale thought to himself. 'These two travellers couldn't be more different. The old man with his wrinkles and the pudgy, round-faced youngster with dimples. The old man looks like the typical Englishman travelling abroad. And that must be his grandson with him – he must be ten, eleven years old, perhaps?' Tyndale pondered and then continued to listen in on the old man's conversation.

'It really has been hard to imagine all the changes that have happened in my lifetime,' the old man declared, plodding along, a few coins clinking noisily in his pockets. 'When I was born the world seemed more settled, more at rest. Now, with the new ideas, the rebirth of Greek and Roman learning, it's different. It's more like a pot boiling over on the fire, hissing, spitting and steaming. It's sheer craziness, that's what it is – so much change all at once. How come there's so much upheaval and change all at the same time?'

He paused, looking down at his grandson's white, pudgy face and bewildered eyes, blinking dolefully at him.

'Oh, don't worry – you don't have to answer that.' He caught himself quickly. 'Oh, but listen to me, rambling on about the way the world was and how I liked it better. What an old man I am. Yes, I know, pretty soon I'll be telling you I walked uphill both ways to school – don't believe me. And I'm sorry – I shouldn't be going on and on about things that can't possibly interest you. So, how do you like our trip so far?'

'It's amazing, grandfather. I love it. But what ideas are you talking about? I'm in school and I hear things. What's going on?' the boy asked, puzzled. He loved his grandfather's way of spinning an entrancing story out of just about anything.

The old man straightened up a little.

'Well, it's hard to put into schoolboy's language,' he said. 'But it began in those places where men like Erasmus and Colet and even Sir Thomas More studied.'

'Sir Thomas More?' the boy interrupted. 'I've heard of him. He's in government at court, isn't he?'

'Hey, they do teach you a lot in school these days.'

The young lad grinned, pleased by the compliment, as his grandfather continued with the tale.

'It began in the universities where ideas began to grow up – different and new ideas, although some of the ideas were actually very, very old, ideas which had been thought up by the Greeks and the Romans, people who lived hundreds and hundreds of years ago. But now, all of a sudden, men in the universities were rediscovering that some of those ideas were very good. But you know how, when you get too many good ideas at the same time you feel both excited and scared? You get too many ideas in your head and you can't keep up with them.'

'Yes, and it's fun but your head is spinning.'

'Well, yes, it's a little like that. The world's head has been spinning with all the ideas.'

'Hmmm,' said the boy. 'When did all this spinning begin?' he asked.

'Well, now that's a good question and hard to answer,' the old man said. 'But it's a little bit like the yeast in that bread shop we just passed. You know how you put bread in the oven – you've probably seen your grandmother do it – you put it in and a couple of hours later you come back and it has risen up? You don't know exactly when it rose – it was rising gradually. Well, the change and the ideas have been a little bit like that. The bread has been rising for some time now.'

'Is it done rising yet?' the boy asked.

'I'm not sure, but I don't think so,' said the man.

'But all your talk about bread is making me hungry again,' the boy said, rubbing his tummy.

His grandfather laughed. 'But I will tell you of one thing that has made a tremendous difference. It is the printing press that has helped move all the change along because ideas can now spread more quickly and more people can own books. As people read, ideas travel faster. You've heard of Gutenberg, right? ' The old man asked.

The boy said smartly, 'Gutenberg invented the first printing press and printed the Bible, didn't he?'

'Boy, you remember everything, don't you?' the old man nodded, impressed. 'I appreciate being able to tell my story to a youngster with a perfect memory like you. Well, anyway, the printing press has helped ideas to take off quickly, though our country, England, has been slow to like it.'

The boy scrunched his nose into a puzzled expression. 'Why? It's very clever.'

'Yes, yes, it is very clever but I think King Henry and the other leaders are a little afraid of it. They know just how clever it is. They may be afraid the printing press will spread ideas they don't like as well as ones they do.'

'Hmm,' said the boy. He had to think about that.

'Yes, but isn't the printing press good? Isn't it good to invent things?'

'Oh, absolutely. It's very good, but it is like a lot of things in life that can be used for good or bad. Think about a piece of wood.'

The boy wrinkled up his forehead as he imagined the object.

'What can you make from wood? What can you use it for?'

'Well, you can use it to make a fire in the fireplace. You can make a wooden bowl or spoon.'

'Yes, what else?'

'A house.'

'What bad things can you make from wood?'

'Bad things?'

'Yes, bad things. Couldn't you take a stick and hit someone with it? Or make a club out of it – or a cross such as the Lord Jesus died on?'

'Hmm. I guess so.'

'Well, that's how some leaders think of the printing press. I disagree with them. But, in theory, the printing press could print good ideas or bad ones. It could print pamphlets that affirm that God is good. Or it could print books saying nasty and untrue things about others.'

'Hmm,' said the boy thoughtfully. He was gradually beginning to understand.

'Yeah, but they can't just stomp out every idea, can they?' he finally said. 'Just because they don't like some?'

'Well, I don't know if they can, but they can try. Nevertheless, it will not always work. In some countries, like Germany – '

'That's where we are now, right?' the boy interrupted.

'Yes.'

'What happened in Germany?'

'Well, it all began with a man named Martin Luther. He was a monk who noticed that the church had become so powerful that it no longer seemed to care about what was right and what was wrong. This was, of course, not true of everyone in the church, but there was an awful lot wrong with it.'

'He hung something on a door, didn't he?'

'Yes, in 1517. His ninety-five theses …'

'What's that?'

'Well, it was a paper stating what was wrong in the church.'

'What I don't understand is, why did Luther hang his complaints on a door? Why didn't he just tell the bishops or Pope or whoever was in charge?'

'He did try to tell them, but, in his eyes, they didn't seem to be listening. Since it was common practice to put up notices for important things,

Luther decided to try to communicate in that way. That was in 1517.'

'That wasn't very long ago.'

'No, it wasn't. Anyway, the church wasn't too happy about Luther. Though Luther didn't want them to do it, some very poor people began to get angry and fight. Some went in and smashed statues in churches; in other places people actually fought against the government. Luther didn't teach any of those things, but some people let things get out of control. There were a lot of reasons those things happened. Still, I think that's why the King and the authorities are afraid.'

It was just at this point that the man and the boy turned down a street. Tyndale, who had to go straight on, watched the child's tousled hair and the old man's thick, bushy grey hair now disappear around the corner. Tyndale sighed, 'And just when the story was getting good.'

Tyndale now continued to walk until finally, after a few hours, he began to feel tired. He dropped his heavy, worn trunk down next to a stone wall and rested his aching feet.

Finally he made his way from there to Hamburg, where he decided to unpack and find lodgings. On the first street he crossed there was a nice little inn, with white shuttered windows and a few window boxes of bright yellow flowers and cascading vines. Perfect.

After entering and paying for a few nights' stay, Tyndale strolled out into the street to take a look around and explore the town with its small streets, quaint architecture, low-beamed ceilings and wide doors.

What he really needed, though, was a printer. He walked briskly down a back street. There was a bakery, a smithery, and a barrel-maker but no printer. He tried the next street. An inn, a pub, a church, a few houses – no – nothing here either.

Maybe he just needed to search after a good night's rest. The sun was dipping low. Returning to his inn, he had a small late dinner and went to bed early. The following day he rose early to a golden sun just blinking over the horizon. It crept up past the east end of town, climbing slowly. Once again he set himself to the task of tracing his way back through the streets he had not yet covered, trying to find a printer.

He made it his practice all day, every time he saw an inn, to go in and ask about printing.

At the first – 'Sir, there, can you tell me? I have some work I would like printed. Are there any printers in this town?'

'No, not much of that here.'

At the second one – 'Not on this street.'

At the third it was the same story. And the fourth. And the fifth, and so on.

Quaint city, but the answer was always the same – virtually no printers. There were some printers, but not all of them seemed like they would work for his needs at this time. Finally, Tyndale sat down, exhausted, leaning his back against a thin stone wall and trying to rub a cramp out of his right foot. 'For all Hamburg's strengths,' he thought, 'it certainly does not have much in the way of printing.' This town was simply no good for what he needed to do and he decided, therefore, to move on.

'Try Cologne,' one crusty old man in a bookshop said. 'They have lots of printing there.'

'Thanks,' he said, and decided it was worth a try.

'Maybe – pretty soon,' he told himself, he might be sending copies into England. There was a lot of work to be done first, though. Still, God's work was better than anyone else's. Just as he said this, for a split second, the ploughboy flashed into Tyndale's mind. He could still see the steady, hardworking hands, the brown, weathered face, the tough, calloused skin. He had to remember them – men like that needed God's Word.

On the Run

Tyndale meanwhile had visited Wittenberg for a short time. Then, he moved on both from Hamburg and Wittenberg to the city of Cologne. The year was 1525.

Cologne was a city which sat on the River Rhine, the third largest river in Europe, after the Volga and the Danube, asserting itself as one of Germany's important cities. Founded by the Romans, Cologne boasted one of the largest cathedrals in the region. Tyndale stood underneath its gigantic Gothic face with its lacy architecture and intricate detail. It was immense.

Still, Tyndale's mind was much more concerned with finding a printer and he began to make his way along.

'Hey, why don't you try a few streets down that way?' one husky, big-chested man pointed, when Tyndale stopped him on the street to ask. 'A gentleman named Peter Quentel, I think.'

He brightened at the suggestion. This was more than he'd found in Hamburg. At least it was a lead.

Following the directions he was given, he found the sign, a simple white one which hung over a wooden door. Tyndale looked over the shop underneath it, then opened the door and went in.

Sure enough 'everything printing' hit his senses at once – the smell of fresh ink, the sight of the printing press standing like a great monument in the centre of the shop, the tap of footsteps and the clacks and thumps and general bedlam of noise. Tyndale stepped in and ran his hand admiringly along the thick, smooth printing press.

'It's beautiful,' he said, smiling.

The man in the shop looked over. 'She does her work, that press. Earns her keep, no question about it. She can pound out work like nobody's business. But,' he said, 'more to the point, what have you got for me? I assume you came because you want me to print something for you?'

'You're right. I do, sir,' said Tyndale. 'How much work do you do for England?'

'I do some. Truth is, I just print what someone will pay me for. What kind of work is it?' Peter Quentel smiled.

'Well, it's not exactly looked on well in England,' Tyndale admitted. 'But there are plenty of people interested in buying it.'

'Oh, illegal work; why didn't you say so? Don't worry about us – I'll print whatever there's money for. I'm a businessman, not a priest. Smuggled books, eh?'

'Hopefully,' Tyndale said, still smiling.

'Well, you tell me who pays and when, and I'll do the work. What you do with your work afterwards is your business,' Quentel said. And, negotiating a fee, they shook hands.

William Tyndale knew the work would go forward, for besides having a printer now, he also had an assistant for his work, William Roye. When he had first met Roye in Wittenberg, Tyndale was very impressed with him. Roye could speak well, was smooth, polished and maybe even a little suave. Tyndale had smiled nicely at him.

'Nice to meet you.'

'And you.'

'I'm looking for someone to help me translate and I hear you are looking for a job,' Tyndale said.

'Yes, I would very much like to be involved. I can provide you with recommendations, and some sample work.' Roye had glossed beautifully, smoothing his perfect hair and smiling.

Tyndale had looked the work over. He was impressed. 'Hired,' he said, smiling. 'Be at the house tomorrow and we'll dig in.'

Tyndale had thought Roye would be a good assistant. However, over the time Tyndale had worked with him thus far, Tyndale found Roye harder and harder to get along with.

Roye had come to work bright and early the first day. By week two he was a little less bright and charming. By weeks three and four he was a little nasty even.

Sometimes Tyndale thought he would pull out every one of his own beard hairs if he had to work with him another day.

Later Tyndale would describe Roye as a crafty man in meeting a new person, with a tongue that could deceive the wisest person in the world. But, Tyndale bit his tongue, because, for all Roye's personality quirks and flaws and as hard as he was to talk to, Roye did the work. And the work always came first in Tyndale's mind and heart.

The weeks wore on and they pored over the text, backs tight, heads scrunched down, wrestling with and pulling out the exact meaning of words, looking at each word very carefully, trying to get each one just right.

'Which word is more accurate here?' Roye asked.

'This one, definitely this one.' Tyndale pointed.

After a few weeks they had finished the translation work up to Chapter 22 of the book of Matthew in the New Testament.

Tyndale stopped by Quentel's that day.

'How is the work going?' he hollered in.

But he could see for himself.

The printing press hummed and clicked. Printhands walked about, sticking letters into frames. They selected each letter, careful not to make mistakes since every error would print on every copy. They pushed the letters into the forms, or holders, and lined them up. A loud thump of the 'form' coming down on the press stone followed next. The words were being squeezed by the bar which held the final block pushing the ink to the form. Just then, Tyndale walked closer and leaned nearer to the ink-stained press for a better look.

'Don't get in the way, please,' said one man. 'We've got to get this done here.'

Tyndale stepped back to watch the whole thing —the thump of the press, the damp, cold, smell of ink coming from the ingenious invention that had saved people thousands of hours since it had been made. Printing was fascinating.

'I don't know what we'd do without that machine,' Tyndale said.

'Probably the same thing they did for thousands of years – copy by hand and break our backs leaning over desks,' a printhand replied.

'Gutenberg's father was a scribe. You knew that, didn't you?' another one said.

'Absolutely,' Tyndale answered. 'That's part of what makes the whole thing so interesting.'

Tyndale could picture it, even as he stood there: Gutenberg as a small child coming down the rickety narrow stairs from his bedroom loft, peeking down at his father hand-copying manuscripts again and again. Tyndale could almost hear him rap his fist down hard on the table when he made a mistake. He would then rub his sore neck before lifting a new sheet to start a page all over again. First he'd have to dip his pen into the inkwell, and then begin the painstaking process of writing every letter individually by hand. Tyndale felt frustrated just thinking about it.

When, Tyndale wondered, had Gutenberg first thought of making a machine to do it? Had he been lying in bed one night, with the moon in the window making him think dreamy faraway thoughts? Or was he watching his father in bed with a particularly bad back pain? Or was he – as rumour told the story – watching the pressing of grapes to make wine when he thought of using that very idea to make letters and books instead?

Tyndale knew dreams could come to you just about anywhere. What counted was that you knew which ones were important. And it mattered that you did something with those. Doing something with those could make the lives of those around you better for years and years to come.

Tyndale leaned in again more closely and got another good whiff of the ink.

'Mr Tyndale,' the big, barrel-chested man warned again impatiently, poking him. 'I must ask you to step back a little.'

'Yes, yes of course,' he said apologetically and watched from a little further away by the door.

'Here,' the man said more kindly. 'Keep yourself out of trouble – go and look at the first sheets.' He pointed to where they were lying. 'Up to Matthew 22. Just printed.'

Tyndale stared with his mouth open. The first prints of his work that he had ever seen.

'Amazing,' he said in an awestruck voice as he looked down at the ink. Just like the ink, he thought, that had asked him to appear before John Bell so many years ago, yet how strangely different. John Bell's writing had been done by hand and sent to one man. This work was done by machine to be sent to many people. That letter had—by implication—stood against any English translation. This printing was for it – for the ploughboy and the commoner, for the average man, the peasant, and the wealthy, for rich and poor alike.

'You look pretty happy,' Quentel smiled as he looked at Tyndale's face.

'Is it that obvious?' Tyndale looked down and turned a little red. The place erupted into laughter.

Finally Tyndale left the shop. He went up the street, whistling his way to the Barnesguild Inn, not far from there. The excitement of seeing his first printed translation had given him an appetite. The inn's green sign with gold trim stuck out on a black, wrought iron post and hung a little low. If you were taller than six feet, it was anybody's guess whether or not you'd hit your head on the way in if you weren't careful. Tyndale ducked his head to enter.

Sitting down at a thick, sturdy wooden table to the clanging of large pewter mugs, he was just about to order some food – anything meaty, he thought – when the shadow of a man standing in front of him blocked his light.

Tyndale looked up, a little startled. He knew the man, but had never seen his eyes look so serious nor his voice sound so grave and low.

'What is it?' Tyndale questioned quickly. His heart gave a little jump.

'Come with me,' the man said urgently, in a thin baritone whisper. 'Now.'

'What is it?' Tyndale repeated, rising instantly.

'No time,' the man begged in a voice which was almost squeaking. 'Please come now, *William*.'

Something about the man's face told Tyndale not to ask any more questions. But questions thundered in his mind.

Tyndale had not yet ordered any food and they left the inn without saying a word.

Having left, the man now whispered furtively.

'Walk quickly, William, quickly. I will tell you on the way to your house,' he hissed.

The man looked around. No one was in earshot.

'What? What is it? I can see you are shaking. Tell me. What is it?' Tyndale said desperately.

'They have discovered you and your work of translation,' the man said.

'WHAT?'

Tyndale felt like a thousand fires had exploded in his mind all at once.

'WHAT?'

'Yes, you are found – you are betrayed and you must leave Cologne at once. I will tell you as much as I can on the way back to your house, but you cannot waste one second or they will grab you. The man's name is Johann Dobneck. Cochlaeus is his nickname. He heard word of your printing along the grapevine and has been working away, layer after layer, trying to piece together bits of conversation in order to find out what was going on. He finally got close enough to actually invite some of the workmen from Peter Quentel's to a dinner last night and gave them more than a little wine.'

'But I just saw them.'

'Oh, I don't think the workers even knew he was on the other side. I don't think they knew they were betraying you. But still – they told everything.'

Tyndale quickened his pace.

The man continued with him, walking briskly. 'They tell me Hermann Rinck is on his way right this second to Quentel's workshop. But here we are at your place. I can't talk any more because you need to get out of here fast, William, and I shouldn't be seen here. Run. Run like the wind, and God help you,' he said, grabbing his arm. There was no time. The man simply darted past the door and then crept down a back alley and disappeared.

For his part, Tyndale burst in the door of his apartment.

'Hurry,' he hollered at Roye. 'We are betrayed.'

'Where? What? How?' Roye turned towards William, confused and flustered.

'Hurry, there is no time. We'll go to the River Rhine. That will get us out of here fast. We can decide what to do next on the boat.'

Roye scooped up what he could, grabbing some papers, and clutching them like they would sprout wings and fly. They scarcely said a word to one another, running out of the back door and slamming it shut behind them.

Footsteps clattered behind them, but they kept moving. 'Don't look up,' said Tyndale. 'Don't look suspicious. Make them find us.'

Moments later the footsteps disappeared and they finally reached the boat. Roye was panting hard, his chest heaving. Turning to Tyndale, he demanded to know what had happened.

'Bragging,' Tyndale said, leaning back against the port side of the boat. 'Quentel's men were wined and dined last night and said a bit more than they should have. A little wine and a lot of bragging – they began to brag that all of England would soon be Lutheran.'

Roye gasped. 'They said that?'

'Yes.'

'So much for secrets.'

'There's more. They bragged that three thousand copies of the Lutheran New Testament now translated into English had already gone to press. Why would you tell anyone that? You can be sure that Peter Quentel is answering for it now.'

'Do you know who will be dealing with him?'

'Hermann Rinck.'

'Hermann Rinck,' Roye said sardonically. 'He's a friend of King Henry's. Do you think they will kill Quentel?'

'Hard to say. I hope not.'

'What about the printing? Do we have some of it?'

'Yes, that's the good part. I have the first printed sheets right here. Thank God, we got them all. God's work isn't lost,' Tyndale said, patting them, then holding up the woodcut of Matthew next to the text.

'Up to Matthew 22.' Tyndale smiled wanly. Though he was tired, he remained grateful. 'The words of our Lord Christ. '

The boat underneath them swayed up the river.

'Has anyone seen us?' Roye asked.

'Not that I know of,' Tyndale answered. 'Although I can't be sure. But for now we have some time to rest, so let us do just that.'

Tyndale tried to slow the terrible thundering of his heart. He had never been this close to being caught. It was an awful thought.

Finally, after some time, the boat stopped at the town of Worms.

'Ah, here we are,' said Tyndale, 'Luther's ground. Let's get off here and try to start again.' Though he spoke calmly, still he looked around suspiciously, watching keenly to see if anyone had followed them. A large man got off the boat as did a thin, angular man. The two men did not look in their direction. Tyndale and Roye both hoped it was safe. It was very hard to tell.

That night, having found an inn, they both slept a little restlessly.

Still, by the following morning Tyndale rose, a little tired but ready to start work in a new city.

Once again he was determined to get a feel for the place, hoping this might be his new home.

Luther's Town

It was a beautiful, crisp morning, the air cool and the sky cloudless and bright blue. Setting off down a sleepy, narrow street and making his way through the city, he wasn't sure why he felt good about things. Maybe it was the quick escape they had made just yesterday. Maybe it was a night of even half sleep. More likely, he thought, it was knowing that this was the place in which Luther had met and debated for so many of the things that were good and right. Whatever it was, Tyndale felt there was something about Worms, something that was different. Something that made one feel, if only for the moment, things would be all right. But Tyndale knew he still had to keep his wits about him.

As he passed down one of the streets he encountered a man who was hammering out horseshoes. Tyndale watched as the hammer swung down hard and made a loud thwump. He heard it ting as metal hit metal. Tyndale stopped and watched for a few moments. He was hoping to get a sense of the town from the people who lived and worked there.

Finally after a last thwack and a whalloping thump to the piece of metal in front of him, the loud clanging stopped. Tyndale shuffled his feet, then began a conversation.

'So much has happened in your city in the last couple of years, hasn't it?' he said.

'Oh, you must be a newcomer to the town,' the man smiled. 'But you are right – much has happened,' he replied. He continued working but not so loudly so that he couldn't continue this conversation. The horseshoe glowed deep orange as he worked at the shaping and finishing.

'I understand the Diet of Worms was here. What was that all about?' Tyndale wanted to hear what the townspeople thought of it.

'Oh – you mean when Luther was called to meet with the church officials and asked to answer for his beliefs?'

'Yes, that's exactly what I mean.'

'Well,' said the man thoughtfully, 'for the most part I ply my trade and keep my head down. I never thought I would care about something like that. Still, it was ….' He searched for the right word. 'I was going to say exciting, but that's not the right word.' He paused again. 'Important. Very, very important. The whole Catholic Church was against him and he wouldn't budge. I was impressed.'

'Couldn't have been easy,' Tyndale remarked.

'No, I agree. I'm sure it wasn't.'

'Don't you think Luther must have been wrong if so many church leaders were against him?' Tyndale wanted to see what the man would say.

'No, I don't think that. I think Luther was right.'

'On what?'

'On a lot of things. But most importantly on whether or not God saves people by what they do or by what Christ did. The Bible teaches it is Christ's work on the cross and our faith and belief in what he did and not our works which save us.'

'Well, it certainly is very interesting,' Tyndale said without expression. What he wanted to say was an enthusiastic and warm 'Good. Then I will see you in heaven someday,' but he couldn't. He had secrets to keep.

'Well, I should let you get back to your work. Thanks for your time,' Tyndale finally said.

'Yes, nice chatting with you,' the man said, as he returned to banging out horseshoes in the glowing hot fire.

The sound of the clanging died out as Tyndale continued on his way. He couldn't afford to stand chatting all day as he still had to find a printer, but he couldn't resist spending just a few minutes at the church in which Luther had stood up to almost everyone.

It was a simple but beautiful church. Tyndale had seen grander buildings, but it was a place he would never forget, not as long as he lived, simply for what had happened here.

He looked around now at the wooden pews which were empty. This would have been where the church authorities challenged Luther. Tyndale let his mind drift, picturing the scene, not that long ago …

'Take back everything you have said,' a robed bishop demanded.

Luther unflinchingly met his gaze, 'If convinced by the Bible or sensible logic that I am wrong, I am willing and ready to take back any error and will be the first one to throw my books into the fire. But, if not, I will not take back what I have said, because to go against your own conscience is neither right nor safe. No, I will not take back anything I have said.'

What followed must have been complete silence or a very loud uproar, Tyndale thought. Anything in between those two would hardly have made any sense.

He looked around again. He wished he could have been there. The darkly stained wooden pews, which took up more than one wall, looked uncomfortable enough to make everything from the waist down fall asleep. But Tyndale knew no one had been asleep that day. It had been one of those important life-changing moments. He smiled. Even so, he needed to get going for he had work to do, God's work pressing in on him, just like Luther. He left, letting the thick wooden door close behind him.

Later that afternoon he found a printer, negotiated a fee and he and Roye began work in the city of Worms, picking up just where they had left off.

Often Tyndale would stop by the press and pick up the latest prints to proofread them and check them for errors. But the work wasn't finished yet. He looked down at the copy in front of him and read the following words:

'Though I spake with the tongues of men and angels, and yet had no love, I were even as sounding brass: as a tinkling cymbal (1 Corinthians 13) and

'I am the good shepherd. The good shepherd giveth his life for the sheep' (John 10:11). The prose flowed smoothly, like honey, but talked to the common man. Tyndale smiled. He had worked very hard at that.

Days went by, then weeks, then months and then came the day when the entire New Testament was scheduled to come off the printing press. William had waited so long for that day. As he entered the shop that morning, he could hear the hiss of the paper passing through the printer's hands, the clamp and clack of the form as it came down and made an impression on the paper. Though he had never had a favourite smell before, now he had – the smell of fresh ink. Six thousand copies! The entire New Testament! The year was 1526. Tyndale couldn't believe it. Six thousand copies. He thanked God again and again.

One day, not long after, Tyndale had a visitor. By now Tyndale had begun to translate the Old Testament, when a knock came at the door. Opening the door, Tyndale found himself looking at a familiar face. 'Robert! Robert!' he shouted. 'Well, I never! Come in!' Tyndale nearly knocked him over. 'It's you. It's really you – in the real, live flesh and blood.'

'William, look at you. You look good,' Robert said.

'Here, here. Come in. Sit down. Can I get you something to eat, Robert?'

'Oh, William, I didn't come here to eat your food.'

'Here. Just have a small piece of bread,' Tyndale prodded.

'Oh, if you insist. ' Robert smiled.

'Here, sit down. Sit down,' Tyndale repeated himself excitedly. 'So tell me – what is the news from England? Tell me, tell me everything.'

'Well, there is a great deal to tell.'

'All of it, Robert, all of it,' Tyndale replied.

'Well,' Robert said slowly. 'Though I don't enjoy telling you this part, there is burning, burning everywhere. They burn your translations – always another stick in their fire, a fire they can't get enough of. The fact is, they burn your translations like grass.'

Tyndale grimaced. 'It's one thing to not like me, or to burn my books. But to burn the Word of God? Fiends. How low can you get?'

'Pretty low,' Robert said sardonically, chewing the bread.

Tyndale paused. 'Well, by burning it they are doing no more and no less than I expected. If they burn me too it will be what I expected,' he finally said, resiliently.

'Wait,' Tyndale said. 'You look like you want to tell me more. What else, Robert?'

Robert got a wry look on his face. His smile was so big it could have reached from coast to coast.

'The best part, William, is that they cannot burn them all – your translations show up everywhere.'

Tyndale grabbed the chair beneath him.

'You're telling me the Word of God is reaching the people, aren't you?' Tyndale said eagerly.

'Yes,' Robert said, laughing and slapping Tyndale on the back. 'Like the sea, William. It is everywhere.'

Robert laughed again. 'I can't tell you the things I have seen. I have seen wagons pass behind the clergy's snooty faces and have wondered, 'Is William's translation of the holy Scriptures in there? Sometimes I just want to laugh out loud at where the books go and how they get there. But the point is – God's Word is getting through. It comes in on cornships, it comes in with imported cloth, it travels through woods and fields. It is hidden in closets, under beds, under tables.'

'Robert, careful. Someone might hear us,' Tyndale whispered as his friend's enthusiastic voice got louder and louder …

'Oh, all right, all right,' Robert said. 'If you insist I'll calm down. But it is a great day, isn't it?'

Tyndale just smiled again. Then, after a pause of settling down, Robert enquired about his friend, 'Tell me. How is your life now? What of your assistant? How do you like him?' Roye was just passing by the door.

'He's a little sharp-tongued,' Tyndale whispered. 'I wish he would go out of his way to be a little nicer. But we have finished a great deal of work together. I am grateful to God for his abilities.' Tyndale got up and stoked the fire. 'Listen,' he said. 'You are bright enough to give me your opinion. You should take a look at the work tomorrow and tell me what you think.'

'I would be glad to, William.'

But then, after a day's work and fellowship, the visit with Robert came to an end. Tyndale hated to see him go. Not only did he enjoy Robert's company, but he always had that terrible feeling that he never knew when and if they would see each other again.

As Robert left, William stood at the door.

'Goodbye, Robert. Godspeed to you.'

'And to you, William. We are always in his care.'

William stood at the window and watched his friend mount up. It was only a matter of seconds before the horse was gone and the sound of its hooves fading.

Tyndale felt a little empty himself when Robert left and was glad for the irritation and distraction when Roye popped his head around the door and asked irritably, 'Can you take a look at Genesis 5 now? We have work to do.'

As Tyndale sat down and began to lean over the text, though, he thought back to Robert's visit. Robert had said the books were finally getting into England! People were reading the Word of God! It gave him hope.

They worked for hours and hours, until the sun dipped gently down towards the horizon.

* * *

It was exciting seeing the printed New Testament in English for the first time. Tyndale could hardly believe it. Sometimes he had to pinch himself to convince himself it was all very real.

Nevertheless, he couldn't help but wonder how it would be received by the church and the King. What would they think? What might they do? Clearly, they were burning the Scriptures already. What might they do to him, too?

This whole business of politics reminded Tyndale of a giant chess game, except that real men's lives were being played for.

Tyndale was right to wonder—for at just that moment, hundreds of miles away, back in London, while Tyndale was rubbing his tired feet in Germany, the King – Henry VIII – was strutting into his chambers. King Henry was in charge of what was the game of English politics. He was the most important piece on the board and he knew it. In fact, sometimes Henry thought himself the only player on the board. He had an ego to match the size of his middle, and neither was small.

People who had been to the King's palace told remarkable stories of the large hallways, ornate gold ceilings, gilded ornaments and beautiful rooms. 'It seems to stretch on for ever,' one said.

Still, for those who did visit or live in the palace, everyone said the same thing. It was the large, imposing figure of Henry you remembered. He was a huge man to begin with. If you added to that the wide-shouldered clothing and fine, sweeping hats which made him taller than he already was, he was gigantic from any angle. It was a wonder any of him fitted in the mirror in the morning. Besides, he could also kill you because he didn't like you that day. Maybe he thought you were a pawn. Power was just like that. Henry gave the appearance of being all-powerful in love and war ... but if you didn't please him everything could change ... and that was a worry ... for lords and ladies, servants and queens.

Catherine of Aragon, the queen by Henry's side, was worried. After all, in the years they had been married, she had been unable to bear Henry a son, an heir to the English throne, and Henry, who wanted a son more than anything in the world, didn't like it one bit.

In fact, though she was the aunt of Charles V, the Holy Roman Emperor and one of the most powerful men in the world, and had a lot of money to her name, queens who were not able to bear sons were, in Henry's eyes, just pawns – common, throwaway pieces in the game.

In fact rumours had been swirling through the great halls of the palace, echoing whispers of Henry's behaviour.

'Have you seen the way the King flirts with Anne Boleyn? It's a sin. He is married to Catherine of Aragon!'

'He wants an heir to his throne. His wife, Catherine, has not, in all these years, been able to bear him a male child. All Anne Boleyn's beauty couldn't move his heart if Catherine were to bear him a son.'

'But what of Charles V, the Emperor? Can Henry afford to offend him? Catherine of Aragon is his aunt, you know. I don't know if he's thinking of it, but it would be against God's law if he tried to leave his wife.'

Now the second servant ruffled his unwieldy hair and looked around suspiciously to make certain no one was in close range of hearing. 'Ah, but as you have noticed, King Henry does not always seem interested in what is against God's law. Sometimes he seems more interested in what works for him. He doesn't always care what the church or the Pope think either, though he has to pretend. Henry wants what Henry wants.'

'Bite your tongue before you get us both into trouble.'

'You know it's true,' whispered back the second.

'Yes, but no one must ever hear us say so.'

But the rumours about Anne Boleyn were true. She was one of the ladies who were often about the palace – beautiful, elegant, and French-trained. Her face was the face of a perfect china doll, her clothes were beautiful. She spoke well, was well-educated, but most of all she was young and unmarried and might be able to bear a son for Henry ... and Henry favoured her whenever she entered the room, looking her way, winking now and again.

'Ah, Anne,' he said with a sweetness and light that was rarely in his voice with matters of state.

She curtseyed. 'Your Highness.'

'Will you dine at our table tonight?'

Her skirts rustled in the draught of the Great Hall, the hand sewn intricate beading on her lovely hairpiece and on the bodice of her gown glinting in the sunlight, reflecting shimmering drops of gold light dancing across the room. She remained slightly out of reach. 'Yes, my Lord,' she said. 'If you favour me with your request, I will.'

He smiled. 'Then so you will – the King says so.'

She glanced down elegantly and curtseyed again.

'Thank you, my Lord,' she said and gracefully began to leave, though her ears pricked up when she heard King Henry turn to Cardinal Wolsey and say in an irritated voice, 'Now, tell me more about Tyndale.'

Anne dared not stay and listen, so she only heard a small snatch of the conversation.

'What about him? What do you know about this man, Tyndale?'

Wolsey sneered slightly. 'Tyndale,' he said disdainfully again, rubbing the ring on his finger, 'that evil man.'

Cardinal Wolsey smoothed his elegant, expensive clothing and thought about his land holdings. Tyndale was an unwelcome intruder into his thoughts and plans.

'He is a fool,' Wolsey said angrily, scrunching his nose in distaste. 'How dare he go against the church?'

Wolsey was wily and had worked his way to the top. Bishop of Canterbury at age thirty, Cardinal by age forty- four, he was now the highest representative of the Pope for the entire country. It was understood that when he spoke, it was as if the Pope spoke. He hadn't been climbing the political social ladder to be pulled off a rung by a pipsqueak scholar named Tyndale. The King wanted the renegade Tyndale found. Wolsey had to please the King and assure him that all was being done that could be done.

The King now strolled to a window and looked out over the palace grounds, which stretched into formally cut green trees, manicured hedges and perfectly trimmed paths.

'Now, again, I say,' repeated King Henry, spinning around and glaring at Wolsey, 'tell me more of this man known as William Tyndale.'

'Your Highness,' the Cardinal sniffed disdainfully. 'He is barely a scratch on the glass lens of the state.'

King Henry now looked impatient. 'He is a large scratch, Wolsey, and if he keeps it up, he will be a glass we can't see through. What is this about the Scriptures coming to my country without my knowledge? Is the translation good?'

Wolsey stammered. 'The translation is sure to be full of mistakes.'

Henry growled. 'Well, whether it is or isn't, I am not happy about this, Wolsey, not happy. This is illegal in my country and I don't care for people who don't obey the law.'

'Your Majesty is full of insight,' Wolsey gushed. 'If uneducated people read it they will not understand it. They don't have the mind for such things. Tyndale is one of those bothersome Reformer-types.'

'Hmm,' Henry grunted. 'Where does he do such a work?'

'Somewhere on the continent, Your Highness. He has not been found even though we receive reports of where he has last been. He is elusive and devious,' Wolsey said, his eyes squinting with suspicion and mistrust.

'Yes, well,' said the King impatiently. 'He is seeping into my country, Wolsey, and he must be stopped.' The King turned to the door. 'Yes, yes, Sir Thomas, come in. We were just talking about this Tyndale man. What do you have to say about him?'

Sir Thomas More, who had been called in by a servant, now entered the room. Dressed in a clerical cap and robes, More was a bright, intelligent man. Austere and self-controlled, his intellect was both striking and disciplined. He was very witty. 'So, Thomas,' Henry demanded, 'what do you think of Tyndale?'

More shook his head gravely. 'I say, Your Highness, that he has set the battle lines against the invincible church of God and should be stopped.'

The King looked angrily out the window. He was annoyed that this pesky little dustspeck of a man, Tyndale, was intruding, for the moment, against his power of state. 'I say you speak wisely, Thomas, very wisely.'

'Well, he will have to be stopped,' Henry said to More.

'That is that.'

'Yes, Your Highness,' More replied, bowed and left.

'Now,' King Henry instructed, turning to a servant. 'My portrait is to be painted. I need you to brush the dust off me.' He smoothed back a stray piece of hair. Moments later the appointed artist stood before His Majesty, head bowed, knees knocking. 'Lots of reds, royal purples and lavish gold, do you hear?' the King insisted loudly. 'This is the Tudor dynasty in England and I must look perfect, or I shall have your head.'

The artist turned pale. 'Yes, Your Highness. You need not be concerned. I was hired for the King because I am very good. You will make a lovely portrait.'

But his trembling brush had to be steadied and the cold sweat dripping down his forehead brushed away quickly. Henry's threat of execution wasn't a meaningless one. Many knew to their own horror how the King's threats could be acted on. All lived in fear of the King, and Henry's advisors would be terrified at his commands. In some ways, compared to Tyndale's life, Henry's life seemed the 'preferred' life, a life full of riches and power and wealth.

And in a dark house hundreds of miles away Tyndale was working by candlelight in long, moody shadows. Had his life been painted at that moment, the artist would only have needed to use browns and blacks – no rich, royal colours to stimulate the eye. But if the artist had had an exceptional talent he might have captured something more, something that set the two men apart. Because there was something in Tyndale's eyes, something trustworthy and dependable that said, 'Money and power aren't everything. Thinking about yourself isn't the only life there is. It's the ploughboy who really does matter.'

Tyndale's New Testament was not the only thing being smuggled into England. He also wrote a book called *The Obedience of a Christian Man*. This too was smuggled into the country, and even Anne Boleyn had a copy of it.

'Look–it's not out against you,' she protested to Henry when she read the book. 'Here—' she said, pointing at it. 'Look. This book tells all the people in England to obey you.'

'Hrrruumpf,' Henry muttered.

'No, it does – really. I don't think Tyndale wants the people to start a revolution or a war. He only wants the Bible in English.'

'Yes, but Luther may have only wanted the Bible in German – though I doubt it – and look what happened then. I am too wise, my dear Anne, not to know what the possible effects are.'

'Well, you're the King. As you see fit,' she said, curtseying.

'I am,' he sniffed royally. 'And no one should ever forget it.'

The next morning Henry sat pouting on his throne.

One of Henry's advisors suggested a plan. 'If we can't flush the man out, maybe we can flush out his friends or find anyone who is giving him money.'

So, on the King's orders, soldiers were sent to Humphrey Monmouth's house. Humphrey heard a loud beating on the door and a raspy voice shouting, 'Open up. Open up in the name of the King.'

Humphrey went to the door and opened it slowly. Three men in armour rushed in, and began stampeding through the house. One rummaged through a desk, overturning drawers, and scattering papers which now fluttered everywhere. Another smashed a vase, looking for books. The soldier at the door explained, 'We know you knew Tyndale. We want to know what you know.'

'I will be happy to co-operate,' he said. 'But I don't know anything now.'

Finally after tearing his house apart, papers everywhere, drawers emptied, clothes thrown across the room, the soldiers grabbed him and dragged him in for questioning in front of the church authorities.

'What do you have to say for yourself?' one questioner demanded, leering down at a seated Monmouth. 'He boarded in your house.'

'He did,' Humphrey replied.

'You showed sympathy to the Protestant cause. You are accused of helping them with money,' the questioner said suspiciously.

'I gave him some money but that was years ago,' Humphrey said earnestly. 'He seemed like a good man at the time.'

The questioner sneered and looked down his long nose at Monmouth.

'You can sit in the Tower of London and think about whether or not he was a good man.'

'But, Your Grace …' he tried to protest, 'my family. You can't …'

'I can and I will. Maybe you will think twice next time.'

'But – '

That was all. Thus, Humphrey Monmouth was thrown into the Tower of London, the city's most feared prison. Its thick, ancient walls witnessed many deaths and executions, as many prisoners had languished behinds its turrets. Men and women, even children, had been taken into the Tower, never to be seen again. It didn't matter if you were of noble birth or a member of the clergy – you could be imprisoned, tortured, beheaded even, at a royal whim and command.

The wind howled through its thin cracks, and everywhere it smelled of death. It was a grim reminder that no one who knew William Tyndale was safe. Power spoke. When Monmouth was finally released from prison months later he went home and burned every copy he had of Tyndale's sermons. Nothing would ever be found in his house again that would ever prove Humphrey Monmouth had ever known a man named William Tyndale.

Things Heat Up

'William!' A friend of Tyndale's came running to the door of the room in which Tyndale was working. He was half-laughing, half-amazed. 'I can't believe you did it. I can't believe you called him Cardinal WOLFSEE. If I had seen that before it went to press, I would have asked you if you really wanted to call him that.'

'And if you had asked me, I would have told you, yes, I did.'

'But don't you think that ...'

'No, I don't think it was too sharp,' Tyndale interrupted. 'If my words have pepper to them it is not for the purpose of being nasty – it is only to communicate. In the New Testament Christ called the Pharisees painted tombs. He wasn't name-calling for the sake of name-calling. He was making the point that the Pharisees only cared what they looked like on the outside, not on the inside. It was a word picture, not a threat. Words must be sharp, like arrows, to penetrate. Cardinal Wolsey IS a wolf, stealing money from the lambs of the church. He's just like a wolf, hungry for more and more money, taking it from poor people; at least stealing in the sense that he lives off more than one church position at the same time while not, in my opinion, being able to perform all the duties of them all.'

The wind whistled in the trees outside, and a thunderstorm began to brew.

'Well,' the friend said, laughing. 'I still can't believe you did it.'

'I do want people to understand why I did it, though,' Tyndale said earnestly.

'I know. When they read words like this in your works, they will,' the friend replied and began to read from one of Tyndale's works. 'Christ became poor to make other men rich. Love doesn't want everything for itself. If it did, it wouldn't be love.'

The printing of *The Obedience of a Christian Man* caused more trouble in England. In the streets people talked about very little else.

'Did you hear Tyndale published his new book?'

'Yes, *The Obedience of a Christian Man*.'

'I hear it is banned, just like all of his works.'

'I know. Doesn't that just make you want to read it more? They say that the King is all in a dither. I wonder why.'

'I can't imagine! But I still don't see why they have to make the Bible a banned book. Can you?'

The swarthy man looked down. 'No, not really - but I shan't say anything. I like my head just where it is, thank you.'

Henry, meanwhile, had mixed feelings. The publication did state that the government should be obeyed. On the other hand, it had been written by an exiled Reformer who was illegally sending copies of the English Bible into his country. Henry wandered into his chambers and read some aloud to himself.

'*I also showed that kings and rulers even when they are evil*'

'He had better not mean me,' Henry muttered angrily. '*are a great gift from God.*'

'Ah, now he must mean me.'

'*They defend us from a thousand dangers we don't see.*'

'Hmm. I like the sound of that, too. And look how carefully he lays out the need to obey the government. This could help me when I divorce Catherine and marry Anne,' he said to himself triumphantly. Henry was looking for ways to get his own way, as always – even if that meant misusing his old enemy's own words. Henry muttered on, 'Of course, Sir Thomas More doesn't like it much, but the church is unwilling to grant me the divorce I ask for, so why should I care what they think?'

Thomas More, in fact, though not a clergyman, was a strong Catholic, and both he and the church leadership detested Tyndale's work, *The Obedience of a Christian Man*. They fumed over it, calling a meeting of its leaders to consult on how to respond. Sitting around a large wooden table, men in long dark clerical robes filtered into the room, many with disgusted looks on their faces. Thomas More sat in a high-backed chair and blinked. The bishop sitting across the table from More spoke first to begin the meeting.

'Well, Sir Thomas, what do you think of all of this?' he said, wrinkling his nose. 'This man is a blight, a disease, and the people are reading him. What are we going to do with this heretical, self-serving, popular fool, this insidious, spiteful, short-sighted, far-flung illegal translator?'

Thomas More remained perfectly calm, for that was his way. His bottom lip curled ever so slightly. 'What we are going to do,' he said, sneering lightly and pursing his lips, 'is to engage our crafty, illegal friend, Mr Tyndale, in another way.'

'Another way? What — whatever do you mean?'

Whispers and murmurs broke out around the great table.

'Yes, Sir Thomas, go on.'

'Someone has offered me a sum of £5,000 to respond to Mr Tyndale in writing,' Sir Thomas More said coolly.

There were gasps. 'Five thousand pounds! That's a lot of money!' There were murmurs of assent.

'Yes, yes, it is,' said More, his jaw tightening ever so slightly. 'And though I won't accept the money, I will write to drown out Tyndale's voice in England.'

'Write? Do you mean a letter? Tyndale wouldn't answer a letter from any of us,' one said incredulously.

'No, no,' More answered, again coolly. 'My idea is much better than that. Tyndale has written books and pamphlets to be spread through all of England and read by the people. I will do the same — writing books to respond to his criticism of the church. For in fact, if we cannot flush him out with spies, it is possible we can write his ideas out. We may,' his voice lowered, 'be able to win the minds of the people.'

'An excellent idea,' all the priests now murmured to one another. 'Why didn't we think of it before?'

'Yes,' Sir Thomas More said, with an unflinching gleam in his eye. 'I will call my first book, *Dialogue Concerning Heresies*. And there may be more after that.'

The priests shouted and cheered, enthusiastic in their desire to get the better of that upstart, heretical Bible translator William Tyndale.

Meanwhile, in a quiet room in another country, Tyndale worked on.

And Tyndale's work was being read, even in kings' palaces. Henry continued to read Tyndale's book, and Anne Boleyn continued to influence Henry. Finally, Henry decided he might try to win Tyndale over to his side.

'I am beginning to think that aspects of Tyndale may be useful to me,' he said one morning to Thomas Cromwell, a man who was currently rising in government.

'Yes, Your Highness. I have felt for some time that Tyndale's work may be of use to you in this time and for your needs,' Cromwell replied.

Thomas Cromwell was smart and chose his words carefully. He knew that Cardinal Wolsey, a former Chancellor of Henry's, had not been able to get the Pope to agree to Henry's divorce and had been sent off to be killed at the Tower of London. Though rumour had it Wolsey died along the way, Wolsey was never heard from again. Henry's enemies seemed to always end up dead.

'I think the time has come,' Henry declared to Cromwell, 'for us to find a messenger to communicate directly with William Tyndale.'

'Yes, Your Highness. As you requested, I have asked a man named Steven Vaughan to engage in this work for you.'

'Send him in.'

'Yes, Your Highness.'

Cromwell ushered Steven Vaughan in to see the King.

Mr Vaughan entered the room and bowed.

'I understand Cromwell has told you of our need to send a message to William Tyndale,' Henry said, gesturing. 'Since your post requires travel in that area we are asking you to hunt for him and to deliver a message from me.'

'I would be glad to be of service to Your Highness in any way,' Vaughan said, bowing. 'I must tell Your Highness that I may have trouble finding him but I will do my best. What would you like me to tell him if I am able to find him?' Steven Vaughan asked respectfully.

'Tell him,' Henry waved his hand imperiously, 'that the King requests him to return to England. And will assure him safe passage.'

Steven Vaughan tried to hide his surprise. 'Yes, Your Highness. But, if I may be so bold as to ask …'

'Yes …' Henry said impatiently.

'Your Highness, everyone knows you have wanted him dead and even he knows it,' he said, puzzled.

'That is the way things were, Mr Vaughan. Things have changed now. His book, *The Obedience of a Christian Man*, tells the people to obey the authorities and the law. It says I should be obeyed – fully, completely, as the King. And I think there are certain persons in this country who should remember that,' Henry said, now preening the gigantic tapestry shirt that covered his gigantic chest. 'Tell him I will assure him safe passage. He will not be killed.'

'Yes, Your Highness,' Vaughan bowed gracefully. But he was still confused. Searching for Tyndale would be like looking for a needle in a haystack – a needle that moved and didn't even want to be found.

Tyndale, after all, knew how to camouflage himself, to blend in, to stay on the move. Vaughan also knew he was unlikely to find Tyndale if Tyndale did not want to be found. Those who were his friends would never give him up, and the people who were his enemies probably couldn't find him. But however tough it might be to get a message to Tyndale, Vaughan had been hired by the King and would simply do the job as well as he could. On his next trip to the continent he began this work.

He stopped first in Germany, at an inn. It was a small place, with large wooden beams and a low ceiling.

'I know you might not tell me if you had, but have you seen William Tyndale?' he asked.

'No, I might not if I had, but what is it you want to tell him?'

'I need to give him a message from the King.'

One dark, wild-haired man sitting at a nearby table overheard the question and poked his friend in the ribs. 'A message to Tyndale from the King. I think I might know what that message might be.'

'No, it's not quite what you think,' Vaughan protested.

'Well, sir, if we see him, we'll tell him the King wants him – for tomorrow's lunch.' The man guffawed, slapping a large hand down on the table. 'The King wants to see him,' he said and the whole table of men dissolved in laughter.

Vaughan looked annoyed, but left the inn.

He stopped at the next inn on his travels. 'Who's William Tyndale?' The owner replied honestly. 'Never heard of him.'

The next place came up empty as well. 'William Tyndale? Oh, I've heard of him – but he's invisible. You won't find William Tyndale.'

And so it went, inn after inn, town after town. Either the people had never heard of him, had not seen him or they were lying and would not give him up.

Tyndale, meanwhile, continued working hard and long. He had made a decision to leave Worms. For some time he moved about. He stayed in Hamburg again for a short time. Eventually he moved on to Antwerp. Antwerp was a city in the Low Countries. It was reform-friendly. Though not exactly on the coast, Antwerp was very much a coastal town in the sense that canals ran everywhere to it, through it, in it and around it. If you wanted water to get your books out by boat, Antwerp was a dream.

He stayed in the shadows, and hid where he could. Though he had friends, they were loyal to him, and didn't let anyone find him.

One night, however, while he was in Antwerp, with a still, pale moon hanging low in the sky, he was returning from a meeting with a merchant when he heard footsteps behind him. Tyndale hurried up, but the footsteps sped up too. He turned down a corner, but they turned with him. He looked for a friendly house, a place to duck into, when an arm grabbed him. Tyndale panicked and tried to shake it off.

Finally a friend of his, attached to the arm, stepped out into the light and Tyndale breathed a sigh of relief. 'I've been trying to catch up with you to tell you something, but didn't want to frighten you,' the friend said.

'Too late,' said Tyndale, trying to slow his heart once again. 'I thought my heart was going to break loose from my skin.'

'I'm sorry. I didn't want to call out your name, either.'

Tyndale tried to catch his breath.

'Listen,' the friend said. 'I came to tell you that Steven Vaughan, the King's messenger, has been looking for you in the city. I assume you don't want to meet with him?'

'I do want to meet with him.'

'William, it might be dangerous,' the friend said nervously.

But with a determined look in his eye Tyndale exclaimed, 'I know, but I want to do it. I want to give him letters I have written to the King and ask that the King gets them. Please help me arrange it.'

The friend sighed, exasperated, 'I don't know why I'm doing this, but you are so insistent. Yes, of course I'll do it.'

So, after months of empty possibilities and leads that turned out to be false, Steven Vaughan, Cromwell's messenger, was surprised when finally a stranger approached him in an inn one dark evening. Vaughan had despaired of ever meeting with Tyndale, the elusive man, and had in fact just written to the King from the town of Bergen-op-Zoom, that, 'I have looked for him everywhere, Your Highness, but still can't find him. I have sent letters to Hamburg, Frankfurt and Marburg. And I have had no reply.'

He had all but given up.

Now, though, in front of him stood a stranger. He was a tall, bony man with thick, unkempt, wiry dark hair. Vaughan felt the breath of the man first, sensed a presence near him, and turned around, surprised.

'A friend says he would like to meet with you,' the man said flatly.

'A friend? What friend? What is your friend and where is he?' Vaughan asked suspiciously.

'I don't know his name. But if you wish to come, I can take you to where he is.' The stranger's eyes were dark.

Vaughan hesitated. It might be a trap – this man could be anyone – a thief, a spy, a murderer. But the man wouldn't say any more and Vaughan had been searching for weeks. On the outside chance this stranger might know Tyndale, Vaughan said he would go.

He followed the man down a street. It was dark and very hard to see. The spires of the city stood erect and mysterious in the thin light.

Finally Vaughan came out into a field on the outside of the city of Antwerp. A man stood there, lit only dimly by lamplight and the shine of the moon.

'Don't you remember me?' he said.

'No, I don't.'

'My name,' he said, stepping forward from the shadows, 'is Tyndale.'

'Tyndale,' Vaughan said, 'I can't believe I'm finally getting to meet with you. But listen, the King has sent me to ask you to come back to England. Many things have changed there. Thomas Cromwell is the new religious representative. And the King assures you, by his word, safe passage,' he said earnestly.

But Tyndale was no fool. He knew 'safe passage' meant he was in the King's favour for that day. The King could let you back in on day one and kill you on day two.

'The King's mood is like the weather,' Tyndale said cagily, turning. 'Sunshine today, and tomorrow — pouring rain spitting on my head. The Tower of London seems to have a lot of people in it these days. Today you promise me safe passage. Tomorrow the King may change his mind.'

'Cardinal Wolsey is no longer in power,' Vaughan said earnestly. 'Thomas Cromwell is now listened to in government, and he prefers you to many of the others. Things really are different.'

Tyndale noticed that Vaughan never mentioned that Cardinal Wolsey had died on the way to be killed at the Tower of London, accused of treason, which merely meant Wolsey hadn't secured the approval of the Pope for Henry's divorce fast enough. If Henry didn't like you, you were accused of treason.

'I know the King isn't happy with me,' Tyndale said cautiously, 'especially since I wrote the book *The Practice of Prelates* in which I warn him of the 'subtle demeanor' of the clergy. But I genuinely want to live with honour and to serve God and my country. I have lived through cold, thirst, hardship and danger everywhere just to do the right thing.'

'Some people know that,' Vaughan replied. 'Thomas Cromwell for instance, and Anne Boleyn appears to have some sympathy with your cause.' Vaughan's mind raced to convince Tyndale. 'I think they will turn the King's heart all the way round. It's different already. Look – he's sending me to find you. That's new, isn't it?'

'The King's heart is as consistent as a set of twigs in a high wind. It doesn't matter about Anne Boleyn or Thomas Cromwell – most of the church still hate me. Don't underestimate them. No, it may have been a waste of a trip for you, but you can't convince me my life in England would be any safer than this little thing.' As Tyndale was speaking, a housefly had landed on his shoulder. He flicked it to the ground.

'Now if that little fly were me and this boot here were Henry ...' He put his foot out as if to crush it, but didn't. 'My life wouldn't be any more certain than that. I have to stay alive to do the work. So I shall not return.'

'But,' Tyndale now fumbled with some papers he held in his hand. 'Will you give these to King Henry?' he said and he handed the manuscripts to Vaughan. 'These are my answer to Sir Thomas More.' He looked down regretfully. 'If I can't have the King's heart, maybe someday I can persuade his mind.'

'So you're really not going to come back?' Vaughan said, disappointed, his voice dropping.

'No.'

'Yes, well, I will give these to the King. It will be good proof I actually saw you. I really am just following orders.'

'I know, Vaughan. So am I.'

The year was 1531.

Vaughan spun on his heels to go. He watched the Reformer slide off into the night, like a fish back into water. Stephen Vaughan had the feeling he would never see him again.

Henry was anxious to read the letter from Vaughan when a messenger delivered it to the palace. 'Would you like me to read it out loud for you?' the messenger said politely, entering the room in his perfectly pleated pantaloons, silk hose and white damask shirt.

King Henry angrily snatched it from the messenger's hand. 'I'll read it myself, thank you.'

'These are for you too,' the messenger said, now trying to keep his hand out of the way.

'What are they?'

'Sent to you from Tyndale via Vaughan.'

'Then Vaughan found him?' Henry's curiosity grew.

'Yes, Your Highness, but that is all I know.'

Henry leaned over and eagerly read Vaughan's letter. It said: 'I was able to meet Tyndale, Your Highness. He is a brilliant man, but he will not come back with me. Attached is the story of everything he said exactly as he said it to me. I tried to remember everything I could word for word. He also gave me the following documents to give to you.'

Henry read the documents eagerly. But when Henry was done reading, all curiosity had flown out the window and he flew into a rage. 'HOW DARE THIS MAN INSULT MY LOYAL SERVANT, THOMAS MORE?' Henry liked Thomas More and didn't like having him insulted, not even by Tyndale. Maybe it was a good thing Tyndale hadn't taken Henry's word about returning to England.

Tyndale had only said what he believed to be true about the wrongdoing in the church. And it was true.

But never mind truth, Henry was back on the warpath. Now that he had read the documents he was even more ferocious than he had been before.

'Did you hear what Henry did with Tyndale's latest book, *The Practice of Prelates*?' One tall, thin man in the street said to his friends shortly after this.

'With Henry there's no telling,' answered another.

'Well,' said the first, 'The King made all the merchants in England who were found with these books ride through the streets with pasteboards ...'

'Pasteboards?' the second man asked, bewildered.

'Yes, two pieces of thick paper, one on the front of the person and one on the back. Signs, basically,' he explained.

'Really?' the second said, blinking quickly.

'Yes, and the signs on them said, "I have sinned against the commandments of the King."'

'No,' the other said outraged, wrinkling his nose. 'He sent them through the streets like that?'

'Yes, then he forced some of them to wear the books around their necks!'

'Do you mean to tell me the King had his men take the merchants of the city and parade them around the streets with embarrassing signs on them?'

'That's exactly what I mean.'

'He is treating grown men like naughty children.'

'I know. The King is furious that he's not winning the battle against Tyndale in stopping the books from entering the country.'

A third gentleman butted into the conversation, 'You would think that the King would be smart enough to realise that all this chaos is just advertising for Tyndale's books. Everyone knows that the books have arrived now.'

Just then, as they were speaking, a man passed by on a horse, led by the King's men. The horse shook its thick brown mane in the hot afternoon air.

'Isn't that Tyndale's brother?' The tall man now leaned forward to his friends to whisper his observation.

'It is,' the second whispered back in surprise. 'But – why do they have him riding the horse backwards?'

'I heard he was grabbed earlier to be questioned for knowing Tyndale. I guess this is the new punishment. But what's that pinned to his clothes?'

'It looks like a copy of a book. Look, they're making him carry the books around pinned to his clothes. The country has gone mad.'

The persecutions continued everywhere.

Soon Tyndale received a letter that his best friend, John Frith, was in prison too.

'No – not John, Lord,' Tyndale prayed.

He looked down exasperatedly. 'I told him not to go back to England, even though Henry VIII asked for him, for it was too dangerous. Lord,' he repeated, pleadingly, 'I still need him here. Though I know that you are still in control. I will trust you.'

Tyndale then went to visit John's wife who lived in Holland.

'I would not have the glory of God hindered for my sake,' she said bravely. 'I will not have him renounce everything that is true and right just so he can come back to me. God is true, William, and God's glory is what John and I live for.' She had tears in her eyes.

'What happened?' Tyndale asked softly.

'He was thrown into a local prison in England, though I don't know why and apparently no one knew who he was. John wisely asked for the local schoolmaster to visit him. When John talked to him about literature and language – things like Latin, Greek and Homer's Iliad – the schoolmaster realised John was no common criminal and asked that he be released. No one ever asked his name and he never told them because of the danger. Soon he was released.'

'Then what happened? Did they find out then?'

'Not exactly. He went to London to stay with some friends and it was there they found him. No one knows who or how, but word got out that he was back in England. You know how it is – people talk. In any case, a guard came to the door of his friends' house, but John had just left the day before, having received word that they were after him.'

'Then what?' Tyndale asked.

'In the county of Essex, at Milton Shore, they finally caught up with him. Officers of Stokesley, who else? Thomas Cromwell, meanwhile, is working hard to get him to recant. I think he understands that John is educated and very bright and thinks he could be useful in England. Cromwell, as you know, is sympathetic to the Protestant cause. He has even given orders that some of John's friends can visit him in prison, which is not always the way in which prisoners are treated. 'Still,' she said softly. 'He doesn't know John very well. John loves Christ too much to ever recant. At least I don't think he will ...' she said quietly. 'That's my John.'

'I'm so sorry,' Tyndale said sympathetically. 'I must write to him straightaway,' he said urgently. 'We will be praying for him and for you,' he said gravely as he left.

He wrote to John right away.

'Dear John,

I was so sorry to hear of your imprisonment. Whatever you do, don't commit yourself on the issue of the Lord's Supper. The Reformers are in split camps and it will not help our cause or yours. Take care of yourself. We are praying for you.'

But the letter came too late, for Frith had already discussed the Lord's Supper openly. In fact, one of Frith's good friends felt Frith's opinion on the Lord's Supper was so well explained, so true to the Bible and so exact and clear that he asked Frith to write his view down on paper.

A tailor, meanwhile, who knew the friend as well, pretended he was himself a Reformer and lied to get a copy of John's work, and quickly sent it to Thomas More.

This became a perfect way for More to charge Frith with heresy.

'Aha,' said More gleefully and angrily. 'Something to charge him on – and in writing too! This is a good day in England.'

Tyndale tried to get more information about Frith, finding out that Frith had told a man named John Rastell, son-in-law of Thomas More, about Christ and that John Rastell had converted and chosen to believe and become a Christian.

'Ah, John, still witnessing for Christ,' he thought lovingly.

Tyndale also heard John had witnessed to a fellow prisoner who had truly believed as well.

But what William Tyndale heard next broke his heart – that both John and his fellow prisoner were to be executed.

On a dark, miserable day in 1533 John was burnt at the stake. When Tyndale heard of it, he sat at his desk and wept.

A Trap is Set

One sunny day in the city of Antwerp, in 1534, when the clouds were lolling around the thin spires that made up the skyline, William Tyndale met Thomas Poyntz there. Tyndale had discovered that Thomas Poyntz, whom Tyndale had lived with in London, had a business house in Antwerp. Tyndale had also heard that Thomas was inviting him to come and stay there.

'How wonderful!' Tyndale thought. This was very exciting. Thomas had always been kind to him, and it seemed like a perfect place to stay. Tyndale would be with an old friend.

They met there.

'Thomas!' Tyndale exclaimed.

'You do get around, don't you?' Thomas said, grinning and looking him over from head to foot. 'But I must congratulate you, William – the whole New Testament in English!' he said admiringly. 'How did you do it?'

Tyndale just grinned broadly. 'God is faithful,' he said. Then, 'Did you know we did the first five books of the Old Testament too, a couple of years ago?'

'Of course I do. I hear stories from others all the time. You're famous.'

'I wasn't trying to be famous,' Tyndale protested. 'Being famous isn't important to me.'

'I know,' said Thomas, laughing. 'But sometimes it just happens. Listen, let me give you a look around the place.'

Thomas walked him through the English Merchants' House. 'If you do decide to stay with us, they'll take care of you here,' he said reassuringly. 'The merchants will tell you that.'

'Hear, hear! Neither England nor the Low Countries will touch us; we're huge money makers for both of them. If we're not left alone, we take our business elsewhere,' a rotund, jovial man affirmed.

'We're the money glue holding this end of the city together,' hollered another.

'We can even give you some.' Thomas smiled. 'You might be able to actually have money coming in.'

Tyndale's head was spinning. It all seemed too good to be true.

'Of course, we can't ever promise you perfect protection,' Thomas cautioned wisely. 'That doesn't exist anywhere. But still, what we have may be as good as you'll get. We know our way around the city, and I can promise you my men can be trusted.'

Tyndale didn't hesitate. He heartily agreed – 'Yes, yes,' he repeated, shaking Thomas Poyntz's hand so firmly he almost wrenched his arm from its socket.

One day, however, while Tyndale was still living with Thomas Poytnz, a man named Henry Phillips came to town. As he appeared at a meeting in which Tyndale was preaching, Tyndale noticed him right away, for he was handsome, debonair and well dressed.

'I live in Louvain,' he told Tyndale smoothly. 'I am from England originally and believe in the work of the Reformers. I can't tell you how good it is to find people who believe just like me.'

Tyndale went home and told Poyntz about him right away. 'You have to meet him, Thomas. He is a man who seems very eager to be part of the ministry here and of the reform everywhere.'

'William, you hardly know anything about him.'

'Thomas,' Tyndale said reproachfully.

'Well, he is new – and that can mean fresh enthusiasm – and we certainly need that – but it could just be words and nothing more … and then … I don't know … I don't like to speak ill of someone we hardly know but just what do we know about him?' Poyntz frowned.

'Oh, Thomas, I appreciate your concern, but Phillips is eager and willing to help in the ministry and thrilled to find people who believe as he does. He could be a great asset to the work.'

But Thomas Poyntz – without knowing it – had stumbled on the truth about Henry Phillips. Henry Phillips was a serpent in the garden, a wily, cunning and deceptive man and a money grabber, the right man for the job.

In fact, Bishop Stokesley, the new Bishop of London, just weeks before, had sent an envoy – a middleman

– to meet with Phillips and recruit him. That was why Phillips was now in Antwerp. He wasn't here to be a student.

The new Bishop of London, Stokesley, wasn't anything like the old. Tunstall, the former bishop, had been educated and moderate. Stokesley demonstrated himself again and again to be cunning, cut-throat, and ruthless. Stokesley's envoy met with Phillips to hire him to find Tyndale.

'So,' the envoy began. 'Bishop Stokesley tells me you have gambled away a huge sum of your wealthy father's money and he has disowned you.'

Phillips met his eyes defiantly. 'That is my personal business. What is it to you?' Phillips had shot back.

'Is that any way to treat a future employer?' The envoy smiled slyly. 'We need men just like you.'

'What are you talking about?'

'Well, Mr Phillips, I have a proposition for you.'

'I'm listening,' Phillips answered. 'Go on …'

'We need someone to go and look for William Tyndale, the man who has been translating the Bible into English and having it smuggled into our country. Someone …' he searched quickly for just the right word, '… clever.'

'Ah,' said Phillips, catching on. 'You mean crafty?'

'Socially capable.'

'You mean a good liar ….'

'Interested in earning some money.'

'You mean desperate.'

'I see we understand each other, Mr Phillips.'

'How much?' said Phillips directly.

'You have no money, Phillips. Anything I pay will be better than what you have,' the envoy said sharply. 'But you needn't worry about that.' His tone became friendlier once again. 'There is money to be had here.'

'And what exactly is it that you want me to do?' Phillips asked.

'You will be given money and a servant,' the envoy smiled cunningly, 'and will pretend to be a student at the University of Louvain. From there you will hunt, track down and pinpoint the arch-heretic — we have good word he may be in that area. If he is, you will find a way to turn him in. But first gain his trust, then lure him out into the city streets where we can grab him.'

There was a short pause as Phillips considered the work.

'You need money,' the envoy smirked, 'and I don't have all day, Mr Phillips.'

Phillips smiled widely and with great charm. He nodded smoothly. 'So glad to do business with you,' he said, shaking the envoy's hand.

'Here,' the envoy said, handing him the money. 'Now go.'

'As you wish,' said Phillips, smiling, and left.

Thus Henry Phillips travelled to Louvain, an easy travelling distance of approximately thirty miles from Antwerp and that is how William Tyndale met him there.

But Tyndale didn't have an easy time convincing Thomas Poyntz that this man, Phillips, was trustworthy.

'Once you've met him, you'll see.'

Poyntz still seemed wary. 'We have little knowledge of or background on him. But you can invite him for dinner,' Poyntz finally agreed. 'If you insist on trusting him, then I will try to trust him as well.'

When Henry Phillips arrived for dinner, he was very pleasant. 'Nice to make your acquaintance,' he said convincingly to Poyntz. 'And it is a delight to have met William. He serves God with his whole heart.'

'Yes, he does. Our God is worth serving well,' said Poyntz warmly.

They had dinner and talked for hours.

'Well, Thomas, what do you think now that you have met him?' Tyndale said after he had left.

'He seems all right …' Poyntz said, hesitating just a little. 'I just worry for you, William.'

Not long after, Phillips heard through a reliable source that Poyntz had gone out of town on a business trip. He turned up one morning at Poyntz's house and inquired if Tyndale were in. Tyndale was glad to see his visitor and exclaimed, 'It is good to see you, friend!'

'And you, William,' Phillips nodded. 'But I come with some inconvenient news. I had plans to take you out for a meal today, but on the way I lost my purse. It is so inconvenient and there is such a good inn not far from here that serves a very nice meal, a good thick stew, I believe.'

'That is not a problem,' William smiled. 'Here – take my purse and see if there is enough money to purchase both of us a good bowl of stew.'

Phillips held the purse greedily. 'We are fortunate – thank you, William. I'll pay you back as soon as we get home,' Phillips reassured him. 'It is a good thing you do for me this morning, for I am certainly hungry.'

'Me too,' Tyndale said. And with that the two men left to head towards the inn.

Minutes later they tried to enter a narrow street. With no room for them both to go through at once Phillips moved forward, then thought twice and graciously stepped back, gesturing for Tyndale to pass through first. 'After you,' he said.

Tyndale tried to pass through the tight, close space when all of a sudden there was a scuttling of feet and the terrible clink and rattling of armour. Arms grabbed for him and as he turned to run back Phillips was in the way.

Tyndale was stunned – he could hardly think.

'Run,' he started to yell at Phillips. 'RUN!'

But then he caught a glimpse of Phillips' eyes gleaming murderously at him and Phillips' long, bony finger pointing straight at his head.

In an instant Tyndale knew he had been betrayed.

Judas. Judas Iscariot. Just like Judas, Phillips was betraying him. Tyndale gasped. The shock was severe. Memories flashed into his mind: a glass of wine, shared jokes, Phillips laughing at Tyndale's table, talking about the work. All the time Phillips had been lying. Tyndale felt sick; his stomach churned; the blood drained from his face.

He flung his arms out in front of his face and tried to push through Phillips, but it was no use.

Phillips merely squinted narrowly, blocked the way, and looked down at the money in his purse, money he had obtained from William only this morning. He walked away coldly, counting it.

Tyndale just stared. As long as he lived, he would never forget that long, horrible finger, hanging in the air over him like a pointed arrow. Nor the smug, cold, indifferent look on Phillips' face. What kind of a man was he?

In the bright, white light of morning, Phillips' figure now grew small and grey on the long street before it finally disappeared. He wouldn't get much for his treachery – the rest of his life he would remain hunted by people he owed money to. He would amount to nothing.

Tyndale looked down.

The chains now being fastened on his arms were cold and clammy, and Tyndale's heart lurched and his thoughts raced. Would they imprison him here? Would he stand trial? Would they kill him? Would he suffer? Would he die? And what about the work? Would it go on?

He tried to remain calm but his heart still thundered in his chest. If you were human, even if you loved and trusted God with all your heart like he did, you could never be completely ready for a moment like this.

He tried to force these thoughts into the back of his mind. 'God knows,' he told himself. 'Remember – the New Testament is in the streets and houses.'

Finally the guards began dragging him away.

Evil had always been there – very real. It had lurked behind street corners, followed him through dark alleyways, chased him from country to country, but now it had finally come to him, face to face, eyeball to eyeball.

'Get a move on, prisoner,' one guard said gruffly, pushing him forward.

Curious people appeared at their doors now and again, to see this man taken. A woman here, a small child there. One little boy stuck his head out of a narrow, dark green, shuttered upstairs window.

'Who's that?' he shouted to his mother when he saw Tyndale being led away. 'What did he do? Did he kill someone?'

'Mind your own business and get your head in that window,' his mother replied, yanking him inside. 'I don't know who that is and I don't know what he did.'

The child was probably the age of the Walshes' youngest child when he had lived with them, Tyndale thought, wondering if he would ever see them – or the Poyntzes or anyone else – again.

The guards continued to push him roughly through the streets, hardly saying a word.

He was eventually taken, weary and stumbling, to the castle – and prison – of Vilvoorde.

The first time Tyndale saw it, he could feel his blood run cold.

Seven deadly turrets jutted up from it toward the sky. The castle's stone face stared back at him, thickly walled and without compassion. Made to look like the terrible Bastille Castle in France, the place looked indestructible, impassable. Everything about it looked hard.

'Get moving,' one guard said brusquely, yanking the chain which held Tyndale's arms as they led him across one of its three drawbridges.

Tyndale looked back. Walking across the drawbridge felt like walking a gangplank or entering the open mouth of a lion. Weaker men had probably fainted here.

As he passed, Tyndale now looked down at the thick, muddy moat which kept some people out and others in.

He shivered. It was a cold day.

As he walked across the drawbridge with aching arms he wasn't sorry for any of it – not one bit. He knew that he was entering a place where no one cared whether he lived or died, but that didn't change anything. Granted, he was sorry to see this day come, but he wasn't sorry for the work. They could kill his body but they could never kill his soul.

If they threw him in front of the authorities, if they tortured him in the last prison cell, he was determined he would never be sorry. Never sorry for translating the Word of God, for trying to get it to the ploughman and the baker and the little boy who had stuck his head out of the window to stare at him as he was marched to the prison. If he had it to do all over again, he would still do it – he would still translate every last word. He had been called by God to do it and doing the work of God was the only thing worth living, or dying, for.

The year was 1535. It was ten years from the day he had seen the first prints come off the press in Cologne, five years since he had first printed the Pentateuch, the first five books of the Old Testament, and eighteen years since Martin Luther had first nailed his theses to the castle church door in Wittenberg.

Was this the end?

He was ushered to a prison cell and sat there suffering from the cold.

'How is William?' someone would ask Thomas Poyntz when they saw him next, many weeks later.

Thomas' eyes would always drop in sadness. 'I have pelted the King with begging letters, written to everyone I know. I have pleaded with Thomas Cromwell and Lady Anne to persuade His Majesty, but the King himself ignores us.'

'He has chased William Tyndale from country to country, continent to continent and now he has bagged his prey.'

'Yes, William is probably a perfect gift for Henry to give the church. The church has been furious with him ever since his divorce. Nasty man, Henry. He's probably crowing with the news.' Thomas paused. 'If you only knew how my heart longs to help William. Sometimes I feel like my heart will break. Though I must remember he is in the hands of Christ Jesus our Lord, I pray for him always. He must be cold.'

'I know. But remember – whatever they try to do to him, it cannot rob from him his reward in heaven.'

Meanwhile at the palace Thomas Cromwell, who was sympathetic to Tyndale and his cause, tried to suggest letting him go free.

'But, Your Grace,' he protested to the King, 'many of Tyndale's writings might help you now.'

Anne Boleyn tried as well. But Henry's answer was always the same. 'Enough, all of you. He is my prize package,' retorted the King angrily.

In the meantime while he was in prison, Tyndale wrote to the Procurer: 'I was wondering if I could have a warmer cap, a coat and some cloth to patch my leggings and a candle because it is very tiring to sit all by yourself in the dark and cold. And could I have my Hebrew Bible, Hebrew Grammar and Hebrew Dictionary too, please?' he asked.

He ended his letter with the following words.

'And in return may you obtain your dearest wish, provided always it be consistent with the salvation of your soul.'

Eighteen long months went by when finally a man came to Tyndale's cell.

'It is time now. Come with me,' he said, the clink of the keys unlocking the door. The trial for him was about to begin. Tyndale was led into a room, knowing the trial against him was just a formality – he didn't stand a chance.

The charges against him were read almost tonelessly by a priest.

'He is charged,' the priest's voice resonated coldly, 'with repeatedly saying and writing that faith by itself justifies, that faith alone is what makes us right before God and that we cannot add works to faith.'

Tyndale almost smiled. He neither could nor would deny that.

'In addition William Tyndale holds the Word of God to be the final authority in all matters of faith, above tradition.'

'Thank God,' Tyndale thought. 'Yes, I certainly believe that.'

On and on the voice droned.

'In addition,' it said, 'he has denied the existence of purgatory and believes faith is enough for entrance into heaven.'

And on and on and on it went.

Tyndale had put the Word of God over the tradition of man, had insisted Christ's work on the cross, without works added to it, was enough for salvation, and for that he would die. Still, he wasn't sorry. How could you be sorry for the truth? It did matter what you believed.

After the charges were read, the church condemned him as a heretic, then led him out to the town square.

They took from him his priest's clothes, gave him the wine and the bread of communion, then snatched the wine and bread from him before he could eat and drink them. Tyndale looked down sadly; he knew the rules. This was the church's way of saying, 'You are no longer part of us.' Tyndale was then turned over to the state to be executed and he returned to prison to wait for the last day.

Finally the terrible morning came. A stake was set in the midst of sticks and other burning materials; a rope and chain hung from the crossbar, and a pale pink-grey sun rose up over the horizon. Faces of friends, of enemies and of the just curious, had gathered to watch.

William saw the eyes of some of his friends, though the friends could not acknowledge him; he wondered if it had been hard for John Frith in this moment, too. Still, he was ready. He knew that in a few moments he would see not only John again in heaven but his Lord, Jesus Christ.

Led to the stake and tied, Tyndale was given a last word to say, and he said simply, 'Lord, open the King of England's eyes.' In his last moment his prayer remained not for himself but for the work. Then, in one terrible moment, it was over. The executioner killed him first with a rope so that he died quickly and without pain. Then a man leaned over and lit the fire around him to burn his body. This too was another way in which the church affirmed he was no longer part of them. Men, women and children stood around, shuffling their feet. Some were cold, others indifferent, some were crying. Some, too afraid for their own lives, cried at home. The Poyntzes were distraught.

But for William Tyndale the sadness had finally ended, for only his body hung there limply, his arms and legs dangling loosely now that he was dead. His soul, however, had gone to be with his Maker and his God in heaven, where no earthly king would ever seek to destroy him and no terror haunt him. No one could ever hunt or betray him again.

As he had said many years before, 'Though they kill me, I will only gain a better resurrection.'

And so he had. On earth, too, Tyndale's death was not for nothing, as something very unexpected was soon to happen.

England had tried to burn it and destroy it – and even its translator Tyndale was gone – yet still the English Bible went on. Somehow God had changed the King's mind, for God is bigger than any one person or any one man and it was his will that Tyndale's prayer should be heard.

Within the next few years, after Tyndale's death, King Henry made a proclamation.

'The Bible is going to go forward in my country – in English,' he declared.

'But, Your Grace,' a servant replied. 'You have spent so much time working against it.'

'Never mind that,' said Henry. 'Go, relay my message before I have your head.'

'Yes, Your Highness.'

The servant ran out to tell Thomas Cromwell.

'I don't know how to tell you this – maybe the King's gout has gone to his head but he has declared he wants the Bible in English to be circulated everywhere in England and you are to convey the message to all the churches.'

Thomas Cromwell knew the King's mind had been changing on this, over time. Cromwell had been part of that. Still, he smiled. What a moment it was. It was coming to pass.

The servant continued, and Cromwell's knowing look grew as he heard the servant say, 'He has said it should be law that a copy of it MUST be displayed in every church in the whole country. He says the Coverdale version has been declared to be without error.'

'But most of it is Tyndale's work,' Cromwell began to protest.

'I'm only the messenger,' the servant replied.

'Yes, of course you are. Never mind.'

Cromwell bit thoughtfully on the end of his quill pen and wrote something down quickly and excitedly. 'Quickly, man – see that this is passed to the churches. The English Bible is going forward.'

And so it was. Not only was the English Bible not banned, but it became law that a copy of the English Bible should be displayed in every church in the country – the church in Gloucestershire, the church in which the Bishop of London served – all of the churches in which Tyndale had sat and agonized over his work – and even the ones in which he had not.

Tyndale's last prayer had not gone unnoticed by the King of Heaven. And the King of Heaven, King over all, had answered his prayer.

William Tyndale – Who was he?

Tyndale was born in the year 1494 in Dursley near the River Severn. He received a good education in Oxford and may also have studied at Cambridge. Cambridge was well known during that time for its Lutheran ideas and it was perhaps during his time there that Tyndale acquired his Protestant convictions.

In 1521 Tyndale joined the household of Sir John Walsh at Little Sodbury Manor, north of Bath. Many local clergy came to dine at the Manor and Tyndale was given the opportunity to meet with them and discuss theology. However, he was shocked at their terrible lack of theological and biblical knowledge and he admonished a clergyman one day by exclaiming, 'If God spare my life, ere many years pass, I will cause a boy that driveth the plough shall know more of the Scriptures than thou dost.'

But Tyndale knew that people would have to be able to read God's Word in their own language before this would become a reality. This was what led Tyndale in 1523 to leave for London and seek support for his proposal to translate the original Greek and Hebrew Scriptures into English. In a matter of months, however, Tyndale realised that this could not be accomplished in England and that he would have to travel elsewhere to complete the work. In 1524 William left for Germany, never to return.

Over the years Tyndale's work progressed and was also hindered. There were betrayals and raids, attacks and even fire to contend with. But in the end God's work was not stopped. Tyndale's translations were smuggled across the Channel into England and into the hands of the people. These translations also included introductions to each of the books of the Bible and explained the theology and meaning of the Scriptures as well as introducing the readers to the theology of the Reformation.

In the year 1535, however, while living with his friend, Thomas Poyntz, a relative of Lady Walsh, he was betrayed by a fellow Englishman, Henry Phillips. Phillips engineered an ambush on the streets of Antwerp. Tyndale was seized while walking down a narrow passage and imprisoned in the Castle of Vilvoorde near Brussels. After a year he was put on trial and in August 1536 he was condemned as a heretic. Attempts were made to procure his release but the fanatical Phillips did everything in his power to thwart this. Early in October of that year Tyndale was strangled and then burnt at the stake. His last words were, 'Lord, open the King of England's eyes.'

In 1535 Miles Coverdale produced the first ever complete printed edition of the Bible in English. Tyndale had planned to complete the translation of the Old Testament but had never done so. Tyndale's name, however, was never mentioned in the Coverdale edition, even though it relied heavily on his work. This was probably for diplomatic reasons. However, by the year 1539, under direct instruction of the King of England, every church in England was required to make a copy of the English Bible available to all of its parishioners. So, although Tyndale had died, ultimately the cause of Christ was victorious.

Take Five Minutes ...

If you have a copy of the Scripture in your own language then it is thanks to Tyndale and others like him that you have this privilege. Today there are many different versions of the Bible and some are heavily based on the actual work that Tyndale did. The King James version takes 90 per cent of its words directly from Tyndale's translation and the Revised Standard Version takes 75 per cent of its words from it.

Today there are translations of Scripture in more modern English, but were it not for the work of Tyndale and the Reformation you would not have the opportunity to read God's Word as you do. You would have to learn Latin, Greek or Hebrew first. You would only be able to do this if you had been educated. In Tyndale's day only the wealthy went to university. Ordinary people could not afford an education. Very rarely a gifted boy from a poor background received an education but girls did not go to university at all. They were educated at home until they were old enough to be married.

So if the Reformation hadn't happened ordinary people would have no access to God's Word unless it were read and explained by a priest. The Reformation let people hear the truth of God for themselves.

Scripture: Remember that the Bible says in James 1:22, 'Do not merely listen to the word and so deceive yourselves. Do what it says.'

Prayer: Pray that God's Word will enter your mind and heart, and stay there, and that your life will show that you read and obey God's Word.

Take Five Minutes ...

Today you can be on a bus, in a hospital, in the garden and you could be reading the Bible. But before printing was invented books were copied out by hand. This process took a very long time. And it meant that only very rich people could afford to buy a book. One copy might cost as much as half a year's wages. People soon realised that printing was one way to produce many copies of a manuscript quickly. Tyndale realised that God's Word could be printed in this way. That is why when people wanted to stop God's Word they burned the Bibles and also attacked the printing presses.

There are many different versions of the Bible today. There are even Bible story books with colour pictures for young children. Nowadays, instead of taking months to print hundreds of books, hundreds of thousands of books are printed in a matter of days. Ordinary people can afford to buy their own books now and that includes Bibles.

If you are learning about God through his Word and have given your life to him because of Jesus' death on the cross, thank God and ask him to help you spread the good news of Jesus Christ to others.

Scripture: Remember that the Bible says in Nehemiah 8:8: 'They read from the Book of the Law of God, making it clear ... so that the people could understand what was being read.'

Prayer: God may want you to teach his Word to others as a pastor or children's worker or a parent. Pray that he will keep your heart and mind focused on the truth as it is told in the Bible and that you will be faithful to him.

Take Five Minutes ...

Think about a world that doesn't obey the ten commandments, or love its neighbour, or love God, that doesn't know about Jesus Christ. We can see examples of that in our streets and towns. Where people don't know about the ten commandments they murder and steal, they don't love God or his Son Jesus Christ.

Tyndale spread God's Word to others. It is God's Word that has the power to change people. It can change you. If God has changed you make sure that other people are given the same opportunity to read or hear God's Word.

Many tribes and nations still do not have the Word of God in their own language. Some missionaries work as Bible translators in countries where even the languages of the native people have never been written down before. We must support these people financially and with prayer.

All actions have consequences in the present and into the future. Perhaps Christians who ruled your country in the past have ensured that good laws and practices still take place today. But if our nations turn against God eventually the good influences will disappear.

Scripture: Remember that the Bible tells us to spread God's Word. Mark 16:15, 'Go into all the world and preach the good news.' This can be at home or abroad.

Prayer: Pray for those countries who have not heard God's Word. Pray for those who translate God's Word into foreign languages. Pray for those countries who once respected the Word of God but who now ignore it. Ask God to make his Word important to your life and the life of the people who rule your country.

Take Five Minutes ...

Think: How does the life of William Tyndale affect me?
~ The Bible in my life ~

The Bible tells you the right way to live and it tells you about God and his Son Jesus Christ. The Bible tells you to avoid sin and its destructive consequences on your life. But it also affects your life in other ways as it tells the truth about life after death. It tells you how to know if you are heading for eternal death or eternal life.

William Tyndale has affected your life as you are able to read the good news of salvation through Jesus Christ in your own language. It is an important message. We all have a soul that lives for ever – an eternal soul – and it is only through the death of Christ on the cross that our eternal souls can be saved from the punishment we deserve. Christ took the punishment we deserved on himself instead. We must trust in Christ and in this saving work he has done.

William Tyndale did a great work but Christ's work is greater. William Tyndale died as a result of his work but Christ's death is greater. William Tyndale was the same as us - a sinner, a human being. Jesus Christ is God and sinless. Tyndale's life affects you, but it is more important to think about how Christ's life, death and resurrection has affected you. Has Jesus changed you? Has his Word entered your heart? Are you now saved from death to life?

Scripture: Remember that God's Word tells us about Christ's great love. 1 John 3:16 'This is how we know what love is: Jesus Christ laid down his life for us.'

Prayer: Pray that as you read God's Word you will discover the truth of God's love for yourself and that his Word will change you.

Four Bible Studies

1. What do these Bible verses tell us about what God's Word is like?
   Psalm 119:105
   Hebrews 4:12
   Psalm 119:103
   Jeremiah 15:16

2. What do these Bible verses tell us about what we should do with God's Word?
   Psalm 119:9
   Psalm 119:11
   Colossians 3:16
   Deuteronomy 11:18

3. What should we not do with God's Word?
   2 Corinthians 4:2
   James 1:22
   Revelation 22:19

4. What do these verses also tell us about the Word of God?
   2 Samuel 22:31
   John 1:14
   Matthew 24:35

William Tyndale
Timeline

1454	Gutenberg Bible printed
1473	Michelangelo paints the ceiling of the Sistine Chapel
1476	Caxton sets up his printing press in London
1485	The first use of + and − signs in mathematics
1492	Columbus discovers the islands off the east coast of Central America
	First globe made by geographer Martin Behaim
1494	William Tyndale born
1502	Peter Heinlein builds the first pocket watch
1505	John Knox born
1509	Henry VIII becomes king
	John Calvin is born
1510	Leonardo da Vinci designs a horizontal waterwheel or turbine
1512	Tyndale receives his B.A. at Oxford
1513	Battle of Flodden
1514	The first pineapples arrive in England
1515	Tyndale receives his M.A. at Oxford
1517	Luther nails his theses to church door in Wittenberg
	Coffee arrives in Europe for the first time
1519	Leonardo da Vinci dies
1521	Tyndale joins the household of Sir John Walsh
	The manufacture of silk is introduced to France
	Henry VIII made Defender of the Faith by Pope Leo X
1522	Tyndale summoned to diocese on charge of heresy
1523	Tyndale leaves for London
1524	Tyndale arrives in Hamburg, Germany
	Tyndale visits Wittenberg

1526 The English New Testaments arrive in England

1529 Protestants acquire their name

1531 Halley's comet appears

1533 Henry VIII secretly marries Anne Boleyn
The birth of Elizabeth I

1535 Tyndale arrested in Antwerp
Miles Coverdale produces the first English Bible

1536 Tyndale condemned as a heretic
Tyndale burnt at the stake (6th October)
Anne Boleyn beheaded
Henry VIII marries Jane Seymour
Wales and England become one kingdom

1537 Jane Seymour dies after giving birth to the heir to the throne, a son, Edward VI

1539 Every church in England receives a copy of the English Bible

Bible Study Answers

What do these Bible verses tell us about what God's Word is like?
Psalm 119:105 – God's Word is a lamp to our feet and a light to our path. It shows us the right way to go; how to obey God and please him. It shows us that the only way to God and eternal life is through the sacrifice of Jesus Christ on the cross.

Hebrews 4:12 – God's Word is sharper than a two-edged sword. A double-edged sword was a fearful weapon. Nothing could stand against it in battle. God's Word is sharp – it can get right into our minds and right into the centre of our lives. Sometimes when we read God's Word, we are surprised at how relevant it is for us – it is as though it was written just for us on this very day. God's Word points out our sins and where we are disobeying God. It cuts our conscience, making us realise that we are sinful.

Psalm 119:103 – God's Word is sweeter than honey. It comforts us when we are sad or in trouble. When we want to learn more about God and to feel the joy that this relationship gives, we can turn to God's Word, and what we read there will be as good to us as eating something really sweet and lovely.

Jeremiah 15:16 – The prophet talks about eating God's Word. God's Word is like food to our souls. We have bodies and minds but we also have a spirit that needs to be nourished by a relationship with God and finding out the truth about him.

What do these Bible verses tell us about what we should do with God's Word?

Psalm 119:9 – We must live according to God's Word. We must obey it in our day-to-day lives.

Psalm 119:11 – We must read God's Word and remember it, not just in our heads but also in our hearts, so that when we need to know what we should, or should not do, our hearts will automatically want to do the right thing, i.e. the thing that pleases God.

Colossians 3:16 – 'Let the word of Christ dwell in you richly as you teach and admonish one another with all wisdom, and as you sing psalms, hymns and spiritual songs with gratitude in your hearts to God.' We should do just as this verse says. When we teach others and tell them that something they have done is wrong it is important to do this wisely. We should pray to God to show us what to do. We should be joyful when we read God's Word. We should sing it and we should always be thankful to God for it.

Deuteronomy 11:18 – Again, we should fix the words of God in our heart. Don't let them go. Always keep them in your mind. Always love them and always seek to obey them.

What should we not do with God's Word?

2 Corinthians 4:2 – We shouldn't distort it. That means taking a verse of Scripture and making it mean something that it doesn't.

James 1:22 – We shouldn't just listen to God's Word - we should also do it, and obey it.

Revelation 22:19 – We shouldn't take away words from Scripture, missing out bits and saying that some bits are out of date and not to be listened to. All of God's Word is for listening to and obeying.

What do these verses also tell us about the Word of God?
2 Samuel 22:31 – It is flawless. It has no mistakes and no errors in it. There aren't bits which are out of date.

John 1:14 – Jesus Christ is the Word of God. He became flesh – he became a baby and he dwelt among us. He lived as a child and a human being on this earth, the only difference being he was the sinless son of God and a real human man.

Matthew 24:35 – God's Word will never pass away. It will last for ever. It doesn't matter who tries to argue against it or destroy it. It is true and indestructible.

Bibliography

For Further Reading on William Tyndale

Cooper, Rev. W.B. *The Life and Work of William Tyndale*. Toronto: Longman's Green & Company, 1924.

Christian History Magazine, Volume vi, No. 4, Issue 16, Worcester, P.A.: Christian History Institute, 1987.

Daniell, David. *William Tyndale, a Biography*. New Haven: Yale University Press, 1994.

Edwards, Brian H. *God's Outlaw: The Story of William Tyndale and The English Bible*. Phillipsburg, N.J.: Evangelical Press, 1976, reprint 1986.

Houghton, S.M. *William Tyndale, Life and Times*. South Holland, Illinois: The Evangelism Committee, 1987.

Tyndale, William. *Doctrinal Treatises and Introductions to Different Portions of The Holy Scriptures*, 1536. Cambridge: Printed at The University Press, Johnson Reprint Company, 1968.

Williams, C.H. *William Tyndale*. London: Thomas Nelson and Sons Ltd., 1969.

Video:

God's Outlaw, Gateway Films, Box 540, Worcester, P.A. 19490

For Further Reading regarding life in the Middle Ages and Renaissance

Langley, Andrew. *Renaissance*. Alfred A. Knopf, New York, 1999.

Macdonald, Fiona. *Everyday Life: The Middle Ages*. Morristown, N.J.: Silver Burdett Company, 1986.

Historical Note to the Reader

When I read a book, I like to know which of the events really happened. Maybe that's just me, but I wrote this short note for parents and readers who are curious and who like to keep facts straight. Since this book is pretty much biographical fact, this means that most of the encounters happened.

Generally any person referred to in the story by actual first and last name was a real historical person who was represented in the best way we know how with the information we have. The only exception to this is the names listed on the church roll in the chapter 'The Big Meeting', in which the names were created so the church would seem personal.

We had to invent characters to help the storyline or help teach facts about the world then. When we did, we either gave them no name or only a first name. This helps you, the reader, to know the difference. These characters serve an important purpose, however, as they tell us about real events that were going on at that time.

One of the few places in which we, and most historians, have to guess is the issue of who hired Henry Phillips to betray William Tyndale. Like most historians, we represent it as Bishop Stokesley. There are many good reasons for thinking this. There is a good deal of evidence that it was likely he and he was very much that kind of ruthless man. However, we just wanted to be clear and note that it is one of the few places in the book about which nobody in history knows for sure.

In addition, there is a little detective work and guessing about where Tyndale was from 1517 to 1521—most think Cambridge—and whether he visited Wittenberg in 1524, and how many cities he visited in the years after Worms and before Antwerp, that is in the years from approximately 1526-1528 in which he may have visited Marburg or revisited Hamburg. Those are really the only places which were a little hard to ascertain. Since he was trying to hide from everyone, once in a while he hid, even from history researchers.

Hope this note doesn't confuse you, but helps you (or your parents who might understand it better) to better understand the story. We always want to be careful scholars and workers, just like Tyndale!

Thinking Further Topics

Against the tide

The smugglers must have felt petrified, and fearful for their lives, when the watchman approached their boat to search it. It is unlikely that we will ever be in the same position, but there will be times when we do feel fearful and uncertain of what the future may hold, for example, when starting a new school or job, or perhaps when moving to a new place. However, we can be sure that God knows all our fears, even those which nobody else knows about. God is all-powerful and in control of all things so we do not need to fear. Isaiah 41:10

Trouble in Gloucestershire

William Tyndale and his friend felt helpless; their friends were being questioned by the authorities and they felt as if there was nothing they could do to help them, even as their friends faced possible death. They knew, however, that they could pray. They asked God to keep their friends safe and to give them strength. Sometimes we may end up feeling helpless about our own situation or the situation of our friends or family. Even if we can do nothing else, we can always pray. Think of a situation or of someone whom you feel unable to help: pray for them, asking God to help them. Philippians 4: 6-7

Kings, Scholars and Vicars

William Tyndale believed that the Bible was for everyone, in their own everyday language, regardless of how rich or poor, old or young. Even hundreds of years later, we owe a great debt to Tyndale and others like him for us having the Bible in English. Millions of people around the world do not have the privilege of having the Bible in their own everyday language. Imagine having to read the Bible in a language you hardly understand! Pray for those whose works contributes to translation of the Bible into other languages; look up a mission organisation like Wycliffe to give you some ideas. Romans 10:14

The Big Meeting

William Tyndale felt bitterly disappointed when the bishop did not take him on. However, William persevered; he would not quit despite the setbacks. And God opened another door for him to move to the continent where printing had just begun. God used a small incident to open William's eyes to another option. We too must trust God even if things don't seem to be going our way. Proverbs 3:5-6

A Changing World

William Tyndale knew that he would have to live by trusting in God, as his life was in danger wherever he was, but he was determined to find a printer who could print the Bible, God's word, and therefore allow everyone access to the good news about Jesus. William

Tyndale knew how important it was to know Jesus. It's easy for other things to become the most important in our life: friends, school work, sport, social media ... We need to always remember that the most important thing is the good news about Jesus, who died and rose again for us. Psalm 119: 9-10

On the Run

William Tyndale and William Roye must have felt deep sadness at having been betrayed by people they thought they could trust, and were supportive of their work. Our friends may sometimes betray us, or seem to be two faced. We can express our sadness about that to God; His Son Jesus knew what it was like to be betrayed by his friends. God will never betray us, He will never let us down or break His promises; we can completely trust Him. Psalm 9:10

Luther's Town

It seemed as if Henry was so powerful, especially as someone could be imprisoned or even executed simply on his orders. However, our heavenly Father is more powerful than any King or ruler on this earth. Even when we don't understand what is going on in the world around us, especially where we see evil rulers in power and people being oppressed, we know that the Lord is just and is King over all, including those rulers. Psalm 47:2

Things heat up

Tyndale wept when he heard that John Frith and his fellow prisoner had been executed simply for being a Christian. We may well face persecution – teasing, being left out, or worse – for being a Christian. John Frith stood firm in his faith despite knowing what that would lead to. Pray that God will give us the strength to keep going as a Christian even when it is hard. 1 Corinthians 16:13

A Trap is Set

William Tyndale died for believing that the Bible states that we are saved by faith alone, through Jesus' work on the cross. We cannot save ourselves. Sometimes we may be tempted to think we need to *do* something to add to our faith, for example, living a good life or helping at church. These are all honourable things, but we must always remember that we only need to trust in Jesus to be saved. Romans 10:9

About the Author

A pastor's daughter and now a pastor's wife, Lori Rich's admiration for the lives of those who sacrificed themselves for the sake of the gospel drove her to write this book, and she looks forward one day to meeting William Tyndale in heaven. In addition, she loves *The Chronicles of Narnia* and *The Screwtape Letters*, and all things Lewis.

CHRISTIAN FOCUS PUBLICATIONS

Christian Focus | Christian Heritage | CF4K | Mentor

Christian Focus Publications publishes books for adults and children under its four main imprints: Christian Focus, CF4K, Mentor and Christian Heritage. Our books reflect our conviction that God's Word is reliable and Jesus is the way to know him, and live for ever with him.

Our children's publication list includes a Sunday School curriculum that covers pre-school to early teens, and puzzle and activity books. We also publish personal and family devotional titles, biographies and inspirational stories that children will love.

If you are looking for quality Bible teaching for children then we have an excellent range of Bible stories and age-specific theological books.

From pre-school board books to teenage apologetics, we have it covered!

Find us at our web page:
www.christianfocus.com

CF4 •K
Because you're never
too young to know Jesus